C000193365

Blackstone's

Police Q& A

Road Policing 2008

Blackstone's
Police Q&A

Road Policing 2008

Sixth edition

Huw Smart and John Watson

OXFORD
UNIVERSITY PRESS

Great Clarendon Street, Oxford OX2 6DP

Oxford University Press is a department of the University of Oxford.
It furthers the University's objective of excellence in research, scholarship,
and education by publishing worldwide in

Oxford New York

Auckland Bangkok Buenos Aires Cape Town Chennai
Dar es Salaam Delhi Hong Kong Istanbul Karachi Kolkata
Kuala Lumpur Madrid Melbourne Mexico City Mumbai Nairobi
São Paulo Shanghai Taipei Tokyo Toronto

With offices in

Argentina Austria Brazil Chile Czech Republic France Greece
Guatemala Hungary Italy Japan Poland Portugal Singapore
South Korea Switzerland Thailand Turkey Ukraine Vietnam

Published in the United States
by Oxford University Press Inc., New York

© Huw Smart and John Watson, 2007

The moral rights of the authors have been asserted

Crown copyright material is reproduced under Class Licence
Number C01P0000148 with the permission of OPSI
and the Queen's Printer for Scotland

Database right Oxford University Press (maker)

First published 2007

All rights reserved. No part of this publication may be reproduced,
stored in a retrieval system, or transmitted, in any form or by any means,
without the prior permission in writing of Oxford University Press,
or as expressly permitted by law, or under terms agreed with the appropriate
reprographics rights organization. Enquiries concerning reproduction
outside the scope of the above should be sent to the Rights Department,
Oxford University Press, at the address above

You must not circulate this book in any other binding or cover
and you must impose this same condition on any acquirer

British Library Cataloguing in Publication Data
Data available

Library of Congress Cataloging in Publication Data
Data available

Typeset by Laserwords Private Limited, Chennai, India
Printed in Great Britain
on acid-free paper by
Ashford Colour Press Limited, Gosport, Hampshire

ISBN 978-0-19-922921-5

10 9 8 7 6 5 4 3 2 1

Contents

Introduction

Before you get into the detail of this book, there are two myths about multiple choice-questions (MCQs) that we need to get out of the way right at the start:

1. that they are easy to answer;
2. that they are easy to write.

Take one look at a professionally designed and properly developed exam paper such as those used by the Police Promotion Examinations Board or the National Board of Medical Examiners in the US and the first myth collapses straightaway. Contrary to what some people believe, MCQs are not an easy solution for examiners and not a 'multiple-guess' soft option for examinees.

That is not to say that *all* MCQs are taxing, or even testing — in the psychometric sense. If MCQs are to have any real value at all, they need to be carefully designed and follow some agreed basic rules.

And this leads us to myth number 2.

It is widely assumed by many people and educational organisations that anyone with the knowledge of a subject can write MCQs. You need only look at how few MCQ writing courses are offered by training providers in the UK to see just how far this myth is believed. Similarly, you need only to have a go at a few badly designed MCQs to realise that it *is* a myth nonetheless. Writing bad MCQs is easy; writing good ones is no easier than answering them!

As with many things, the design of MCQs benefits considerably from time, training and experience. Many MCQ writers fall easily and often unwittingly into the trap of making their questions too hard, too easy or too obscure, or completely different from the type of question that you will eventually encounter in your own particular exam. Others seem to use the MCQ as a way to catch people out or to show how smart they, the authors, are (or think they are).

There are several purposes for which MCQs are very useful. The first is in producing a reliable, valid and fair test of knowledge and understanding across a wide range of subject matter. Another is an aid to study, preparation and revision for such examinations and tests. The differences in objective mean that there are slight differences in the rules that the MCQ writers follow. Whereas the design of fully validated MCQs to be used in high stakes examinations which will effectively determine who passes and who fails have very strict guidelines as to construction, content and style, less stringent rules apply to MCQs that are being used for teaching and revision. For that reason, there may be types of MCQ that are appropriate in the latter setting which would not be used in the former. However, in developing the MCQs for this book, the authors have tried to follow the fundamental rules of MCQ design but they would not claim to have replicated the level of psychometric rigour that is — and has to be — adopted by the type of examining bodies referred to above.

These MCQs are designed to reinforce your knowledge and understanding, to highlight any gaps or weaknesses in that knowledge and understanding and to help focus your revision of the relevant topics.

I hope that we have achieved that aim.

Good luck!

Blackstone's Police Q&As — Special Features

References to Blackstone's Police Manuals

Every answer is followed by a paragraph reference to Blackstone's Police Manuals. This means that once you have attempted a question and looked at an answer, the Manual can immediately be referred to for help and clarification.

Unique numbers for each question

Each question and answer has the same unique number. This should ensure that there is no confusion as to which question is linked to which answer. For example, Question 2.1 is linked to Answer 2.1.

Checklists

The checklists are designed to help you keep track of your progress when answering the multiple choice questions. If you fill in the checklist after attempting a question, you will be able to check how many you got right on the first attempt and will know immediately which questions need to be revisited a second time. Please visit www.blackstonespolicemanuals.com and click through to the Blackstone's Police Q&As 2008 page. You will then find electronic versions of the checklists to download and print out. Email any queries or comments on the book to: police.uk@oup.com.

Acknowledgements

This book has been written as an accompaniment to *Blackstone's Police Manuals*, and will test the knowledge you have accrued through reading that series. It is of the essence that full study of the relevant chapters in each *Police Manual* is completed prior to attempting the Questions and Answers. As qualified police trainers we recognise that students tend to answer questions incorrectly either because they don't read the question properly, or because one of the 'distracters' has done its work. The distracter is one of the three incorrect answers in a multiple-choice question (MCQ), and is designed to distract you from the correct answer and in this way discriminate between candidates: the better-prepared candidate not being 'distracted'.

So particular attention should be paid to the ***Answers*** sections, and students should ask themselves 'Why did I get that question wrong?' and, just as importantly, 'Why did I get that question right?' Combining the information gained in the ***Answers*** section together with re-reading the chapter in the *Police Manuals* should lead to greater understanding of the subject matter.

The authors wish to thank all the staff at Oxford University Press who have helped put this publication together. We would also like to show appreciation to Alistair MacQueen for his vision and support, without which this project would never have been started; also Fraser Sampson, consultant editor of Blackstone's Police Manuals, whose influence on these Q&As is appreciated.

Huw would like to thank Caroline for her constant love, support and understanding over the past year — and her ability to withstand the pressures of being the partner to a workaholic! Special thanks to Lawrence and Maddie — two perfect young adults. Last but not least, love and special affection to Haf and Nia, two beautiful young girls.

John would like to thank Sue, David, Catherine and Andrew for their continued support, and understanding that 'deadline' means 'deadline'.

1 Classifications and Concepts

Please note that the questions in this chapter relate to material in the Blackstone's Police Manuals which has been excluded from the Inspectors' Exam syllabus for 2008.

STUDY PREPARATION

The classifications and concepts set out in road traffic legislation are critical to understanding and proving many — if not all — the relevant offences. There is little point in knowing that a particular offence can only be committed by a motor vehicle for instance, if you don't recognise a 'motor vehicle' when you come across one. It should be noted that the Police Reform Act 2002 has added another definition of a 'motor vehicle' to the one more commonly found in s. 185(1) of the Road Traffic Act 1988.

The classifications and concepts addressed in this chapter are therefore the building blocks for the rest of the subjects that follow — so they are well worth careful study.

QUESTIONS

Question 1.1

Section 59 of the Police Reform Act 2002 contains its own definition of a 'motor vehicle'.

Which of the below would be the correct description of a motor vehicle under this Act?

A Any mechanically propelled vehicle, which is intended or adapted for use on roads.

B Any mechanically propelled vehicle, whether or not it is intended or adapted for use on roads.
C Any mechanically propelled vehicle, which is intended for use on roads.
D Any vehicle whose function is to be used on roads as a mechanically propelled vehicle.

Question 1.2

ARMSTRONG owns a vintage car, which he takes to shows, by loading it onto a trailer and towing it. The vintage car was manufactured in 1939, and was used on the road until 1970. ARMSTRONG, however, has never used the car on the road since he bought it.

Could ARMSTRONG's car be described as a motor vehicle, under s. 185(1) of the Road Traffic Act 1988, in these circumstances?

A No, as the vehicle is not currently being used on the road.
B Yes, but only if ARMSTRONG intends to use the vehicle on the road in future.
C Yes, regardless of ARMSTRONG's intent as to the future use of the vehicle.
D No, as ARMSTRONG has not adapted the vehicle for use on roads.

Question 1.3

NEWBERRY removed the engine from his car, and arranged for his friend, SIMMONDS to help him tow the car to a garage to have a new engine fitted. They were stopped by the police while towing the car on a road.

Which of the following statements is correct, in relation to the status of the vehicle under the Road Traffic Act 1988?

A It was both mechanically propelled and a motor vehicle.
B It was still mechanically propelled, but was not a motor vehicle.
C It was still a motor vehicle, but was not mechanically propelled.
D It was neither a motor vehicle nor mechanically propelled.

Question 1.4

FLOYD has bought a new motor-assisted pedal cycle and intends using it to commute between work and home, because of an increase in congestion and parking charges. The pedal cycle is designed so that the motor can be used to assist with travelling uphill, but FLOYD can switch the motor off and use the pedals to propel the cycle on other stretches of road.

Would FLOYD's cycle be classed as a mechanically propelled vehicle in these circumstances?

A Yes, but only when it is being propelled by the motor.
B Yes, provided it is intended for use on the road.
C No, because it is capable of being pedalled manually.
D Yes, regardless of whether it is intended for use on the road; and even if it is being pedalled manually.

Question 1.5

The term 'passenger vehicle' is defined in the Road Vehicles (Construction and Use) Regulations 1986 (SI 1986/1078).

In relation to this definition, which of the following statements is correct?

A A minibus carries at least 9 persons including the driver.
B A minibus carries at least 8 persons including the driver.
C A minibus carries at least 9 persons excluding the driver.
D A minibus carries at least 8 persons excluding the driver.

Question 1.6

A 'coach' is defined in the Road Vehicles (Construction and Use) Regulations 1986 (SI 1986/1078).

Which of the following is correct, assuming the vehicle has more than 16 seated passengers?

A Maximum gross weight of more than 3.5 tonnes and maximum speed exceeding 56 mph.
B Maximum gross weight of more than 7.5 tonnes and maximum speed exceeding 60 mph.
C Maximum gross weight of more than 7.5 tonnes and maximum speed exceeding 56 mph.
D Maximum gross weight of more than 3.5 tonnes and maximum speed exceeding 60 mph.

Question 1.7

The definition of a 'medium-sized goods vehicle' includes details about its permissible weight and the number of passengers it may carry.

In relation to what a 'medium-sized goods vehicle' is, which of the following statements is correct?

A More than 3 tonnes, no more than 9 passengers including the driver.

B More than 3.5 tonnes, no more than 9 passengers excluding the driver.

C More than 3.5 tonnes, no limit on the number of passengers.

D More than 3.5 tonnes, no more than 9 passengers including the driver.

Question 1.8

Section 108(1) of the Road Traffic Act 1988 defines a 'moped'.

In respect of a 'moped' first used after 1 August 1977, which of the following statements is correct?

A It must have an engine size that does not exceed 125 cc and a maximum speed of 50 kilometres per hour.

B It must have an engine size that does not exceed 50 cc and be fitted with pedals.

C It must have an engine size that does not exceed 50 cc and a maximum speed of 50 kilometres per hour.

D It must have an engine size that does not exceed 50 cc and be propelled by electric power.

Question 1.9

Section 121 of the Road Traffic Act 1988 contains the definition of a large passenger-carrying vehicle (PCV).

In relation to this definition, which of the following statements is correct?

A It will be a vehicle which is constructed or adapted to carry more than 16 passengers.

B It will be a vehicle which weighs more than 3.5 tonnes and is constructed or adapted to carry more than 16 passengers.

C It will be a vehicle which is constructed or adapted to carry more than 16 passengers for hire or reward.

D It will be a vehicle which is constructed or adapted to carry more than 16 passengers, including the driver.

Question 1.10

LEES had been involved in a long-standing dispute with her neighbour, GREEN, over parking outside their houses. One morning, LEES was leaving for work. However,

GREEN had parked his car bumper to bumper with her own, making it difficult for her to get out of her parking space. LEES deliberately drove into GREEN's car to try to move it forward, to give herself some space. As a result, damage was caused to both vehicles.

In these circumstances, what test would a court have to apply, in determining whether an 'accident' has taken place, under the Road Traffic Act 1988?

A That an ordinary person would think an accident has taken place.

B None. An accident has not taken place, as the act was deliberate.

C That LEES realised at the time that an accident was taking place.

D That a reasonable person would think an accident has taken place.

Question 1.11

CLIFFORD was driving his car and his wife LISA was in the front passenger seat. CLIFFORD's mobile phone rang, but it had fallen behind his seat. CLIFFORD asked LISA to steer the car while he reached for his phone. LISA took hold of the wheel, but the car veered across the carriageway and collided with a lamp post, causing substantial damage to it.

Who may be charged in relation to 'driving' in these circumstances?

A LISA is not liable, as only one person may be the driver of a vehicle at any one time.

B LISA and CLIFFORD could both be held to be the driver of the vehicle.

C LISA and CLIFFORD could both be held to be the driver of the vehicle, provided they are not charged with dangerous driving.

D Either LISA or CLIFFORD could be held to be the driver, but to charge both is not permitted in relation to road traffic offences.

Question 1.12

MICHAELS was driving his car on a road when his mobile phone rang. He did not have a hands-free kit, therefore he stopped at the side of the road. MICHAELS answered the phone while his car was stationary, with the engine still running. The handbrake was unset and MICHAELS was controlling the vehicle with the foot-brake. He remained in this position for 10 minutes, before completing the call and driving off.

In these circumstances, would MICHAELS have been the driver of the motor vehicle, while it was stationary?

A No, as the vehicle was stationary, he was no longer a driver.

B Yes, he will be a driver until the end of his journey.

C Yes, because he was controlling the propulsion of the vehicle with the foot-brake.

D No, the vehicle was stationary only for a short period of time.

Question 1.13

For many offences under the Road Traffic Act 1988, a person will need to be held to be 'driving'.

In which of the following scenarios will the person probably be deemed to be 'driving' a vehicle?

A McDONAGH was pushing his car, while leaning through the window to steer it.

B BRUCE was sitting astride his motorbike, the engine was off, but he was manipulating the controls.

C JONES was the front seat passenger in a car and grabbed the steering wheel suddenly to stop the driver hitting a cat.

D HARRIS was operating the controls of a car stuck on a grass verge with the wheels spinning but with no forward movement of the vehicle.

Question 1.14

KELLY was drunk and decided to drive home. He opened his car door and sat in the driver's seat. However, when KELLY tried to start the car, he could not do so because he was using his house keys. Eventually KELLY managed to find the correct key, but the car would not start, as the battery was flat.

In these circumstances, which would be the first point at which KELLY has 'attempted' to drive his car?

A He did not attempt to drive the car at any time.

B When he tried to start the car with the correct key.

C When he first sat in the driver's seat.

D When he tried to start the car with the house key.

Question 1.15

WATKINS borrowed his friend's car one evening and went out drinking. On his way home, he went to a takeaway restaurant. WATKINS was overheard by CARTER, boasting about driving home. It was obvious that WATKINS was drunk and CARTER telephoned the police. WATKINS was leaving the premises when the police arrived.

In relation to the proof required to establish whether a person is 'in charge' of a vehicle, which of the following is true?

A WATKINS must show that there was no likelihood of him resuming control of the vehicle while he was drunk.

B The prosecution must show that WATKINS intended to drive the vehicle in the future.

C WATKINS must show that he had no intention of resuming control of the vehicle while he was drunk.

D The prosecution must show that there was a likelihood of WATKINS driving the vehicle in the future.

Question 1.16

HILTON took his car to MOHAMMED's garage for repairs. About five minutes after HILTON left, MOHAMMED had to park the car in the road to make room for another car. As MOHAMMED was walking away from the car, Constable DAVIES was walking past and noticed that it was not displaying a vehicle excise licence.

Who would be the 'keeper' of the vehicle in these circumstances?

A HILTON only, as he is the owner of the vehicle.

B MOHAMMED only.

C Neither, as the vehicle was not on the road for long.

D Both MOHAMMED and HILTON.

Question 1.17

HAWKINS was involved in a road traffic collision. HAWKINS was to blame, having travelled through a red traffic light. When the police arrived, HAWKINS told the officer that she was diabetic and had blacked out momentarily, having suffered a hypoglycaemic episode.

Would HAWKINS be able to rely on this as a defence in these circumstances?

A No, HAWKINS has no defence in these circumstances.

B Yes, such an attack would provide an automatic defence.

C Yes, provided she could show the attack was unforeseen.

D No, even though the element of *mens rea* is not present, the *actus reus* is.

Question 1.18

A road is defined under s. 192(1) of the Road Traffic Act 1988.

In which of the following cases will the vehicle be said to be 'on a road'?

A RANDALL parked his van on his driveway; however, the rear of the vehicle was sticking out and blocking the pavement.

B HOPKIRK was driving his vehicle on a lane to a private golf club of which he was a member.

C BARNES was driving down a road to a beach. The road had common public usage; but there was a sign indicating that it was 'Private'.

D HAWKINS was driving to a farm that had a gate with a sign saying 'contractors only', HAWKINS had opened the gate and was not a contractor.

Question 1.19

Case law has often assisted in deciding whether or not a car park may become a 'road' in certain circumstances.

In relation to whether a car park can become a 'road' for the purposes of the Road Traffic Act 1988, which of the following statements is correct?

A A car park is provided for parking vehicles and could not be a road in any circumstances.

B A car park forms part of the highway; therefore will always be a road for the purposes of the Act.

C A car park is provided for parking vehicles and could only be a road in exceptional circumstances.

D A car park with road markings and traffic signs will always be a road, if it has the general appearance of a road.

Question 1.20

VIVIER arranged a Scout fête, and was given permission to use a field belonging to GILES, a local farmer. On the day of the fête, entry was restricted to members of the local Scout groups, and drivers of vehicles were charged £1 each for entry.

In relation to road traffic offences, would GILES' field qualify as a 'public' place in these circumstances?

A No, as entry to the field was restricted to certain people.

B Yes, as members of the public were allowed access.

C Yes, people were using the field with GILES' permission.

D No, as the people using the field were charged for entry.

Question 1.21

TANNER was stopped by Constable CHEN one evening as she drove her vehicle in an access road leading to a block of flats. Constable CHEN suspected that TANNER had been drinking and asked her to supply a specimen of breath, which proved positive. She was later charged with driving with excess alcohol. At a later court appearance, she pleaded not guilty. TANNER relied on the defence that the access road which she was driving on belonged to a local housing department and that it was not a public place. There were signs at the entrance to the access road saying 'Private Residents Only'.

What would the prosecution need to show, in order to prove that the road was, in fact, a public place?

A The prosecution would need to provide clear evidence that the road was used by motorists other than residents.

B The prosecution would not be able to show that the access road was a public place, because of the signs that were in place.

C The prosecution would need to provide some evidence that the road was used by motorists other than residents.

D The prosecution would not be able to show that the access road was a public place, because a private place cannot become a public place in any circumstances.

Question 1.22

RICHLEY was stopped by police officers in the car park of the Red Lion public house at 9.30 pm, and asked to provide a specimen of breath for analysis, which was positive. The car park had a sign up saying 'customers only'.

Is this car park a 'public place' at this time?

A Only if the prosecution can adduce clear evidence showing who uses the car park, when and for what purpose.

B No, as only a 'special class of public' i.e. customers are allowed to park there.

C Yes, even if the prosecution do not adduce evidence that the car park was a public place.

D No, as no invitation or permission was given to the public in general, only to persons wishing to use the public house.

Question 1.23

There are some offences that can be committed on 'public bridleways'.

In relation to 'public bridleways' which of the following is correct?

A A bridleway is always a highway, but never a road.

B A bridleway can, in certain circumstances, be a highway but never a road.

C A bridleway is never a highway, but in certain circumstances can be a road.

D A bridleway is always a highway, and therefore a road.

Question 1.24

BAKER was driving a tractor and towing a trailer laden with hay on a road, on behalf of his employer, RICHARDSON. Constable SHAH stopped BAKER for having an insecure load, as some of the bales had fallen off the trailer and on to the road. Constable SHAH reported BAKER for the offence and later spoke to RICHARDSON, who denied responsibility as BAKER had loaded the trailer himself. RICHARDSON stated he would not have authorised the load to be carried in such a manner.

Would RICHARDSON be guilty of 'using' a vehicle in these circumstances?

A No, as he did not authorise BAKER to use the vehicle in such a way.

B No, as BAKER was not acting in the course of his employment.

C No, as BAKER was drawing a trailer, only he could 'use' it.

D Yes, he would be guilty in these circumstances alone.

Question 1.25

In certain circumstances an offence of 'using' a vehicle may be committed.

In relation to the term 'using' a vehicle, which of the following is correct?

A If a vehicle is on a road and is in an unroadworthy condition, the owner cannot be said to be using it.

B The passenger in a vehicle cannot be guilty of using it in any circumstances.

C A trailer attached to a vehicle can never be 'used'.

D Only if an employee is driving the vehicle can an employer be said to be using it.

Question 1.26

PRICE is the transport manager of a haulage company. He knows that most of his drivers make false entries on their tachograph sheets. PRICE has not instructed them to do this, but as it means that the drivers work longer hours on behalf of the company, he does not stop them. HILLMAN, the owner of the company, is unaware of what is happening.

Is either PRICE or HILLMAN guilty of 'causing' offences in relation to drivers' hours in these circumstances?

A Yes, PRICE only, as he has turned a blind eye to what is happening.
B No, neither person is guilty of 'causing' offences in these circumstances.
C Yes, HILLMAN only as the owner of the company.
D Yes, both people would be 'causing' offences in these circumstances.

Question 1.27

Generally, in order to prove an offence of 'permitting', it will be necessary to show some knowledge by the defendant of the use of his or her vehicle.

What must you prove the defendant knew in order for him or her to be guilty of 'permitting'?

A Knowledge only that the vehicle was being used on a road.
B Knowledge by the defendant of the vehicle's use or of the unlawful nature of that use.
C Knowledge only by the defendant of the vehicle's use.
D Knowledge by the defendant of the vehicle's use and of the unlawful nature of that use.

ANSWERS

Answer 1.1

Answer **B** — The definition of a motor vehicle under s. 59 of the Police Reform Act 2002 is, 'any mechanically propelled vehicle, whether or not it is intended or adapted for use on roads'. This section created an offence of using a motor vehicle in a manner which is likely to cause harassment, alarm or distress to members of the public. The key difference between this definition and the one contained in s. 185(1) of the Road Traffic Act 1988 is that it is irrelevant whether the mechanically propelled vehicle was intended or adapted for use on the road (which about covers any vehicle capable of being propelled mechanically). Answers A and C are therefore incorrect. The description contained in answer D is incorrect, as it has been taken from the definition of a motor vehicle under the Vehicles (Crime) Act 2001.

Road Policing, para. 3.1.2.1

Answer 1.2

Answer **C** — Under s. 185(1) of the Road Traffic Act 1988, a motor vehicle is a mechanically propelled vehicle, intended *or* adapted for use on roads. It follows that if a vehicle is not intended or adapted for use on roads, it will not be a motor vehicle for these purposes.

A vehicle is 'intended' for use on the roads, if it was intended that it should be so used *when it was manufactured*. It is immaterial that it is not being used on a road now and answer A is therefore incorrect.

The test will be an objective one — but it does not look at the intention of the owner (*Chief Constable of Avon and Somerset* v *Fleming* [1987] RTR 378). Answer B is therefore incorrect.

Answer D is incorrect because it is immaterial whether the vehicle has been adapted for use on roads, as it was intended to be so used.

Road Policing, para. 3.1.2.1

Answer 1.3

Answer **A** — Removing an engine from a vehicle does not stop it from being 'mechanically propelled', if you can show that the engine can easily be replaced (*Newberry* v *Simmonds* [1961] 2 All ER 318). Answers C and D are therefore incorrect.

A vehicle that is being towed by another will still be a motor vehicle (*Cobb* v *Whorton* [1971] RTR 392). Answers B and D are therefore incorrect.

Road Policing, para. 3.1.2.1

Answer 1.4

Answer **D** — A vehicle will be a 'mechanically propelled vehicle' if it is constructed so that it can be propelled mechanically. Whether or not the vehicle is intended or adapted for use on roads will only become relevant when determining if it is a 'motor vehicle'. Since the question asks whether a motor-assisted pedal cycle will be classed as 'mechanically propelled', answer B is incorrect.

A motor-assisted pedal cycle will be a mechanically propelled vehicle even when it is being pedalled (*Floyd* v *Bush* [1953] 1 WLR 242). Answers A and C are therefore incorrect.

Road Policing, para. 3.1.2.1

Answer 1.5

Answer **C** — A passenger-carrying vehicle, which is constructed to carry more than 8 but no more than 16 passengers, will be classed as a 'minibus'. (If the figure is more than 16, the vehicle will be classed as a 'large bus'.) Note that this is *more* than 8 — it is at least 9 persons; answers B and D are therefore incorrect. References to passengers do not include the driver for this definition, therefore answer A is incorrect.

Road Policing, para. 3.1.2.2

Answer 1.6

Answer **B** — If a passenger vehicle is constructed or adapted to carry more than 8 but no more than 16 passengers it will be a 'minibus', and if more than 16 seated passengers it will be a 'large bus' (reg. 3(2)). A large bus as defined above which has a maximum gross weight of more than 7.5 tonnes and having a maximum speed exceeding 60 mph is a 'coach'. Applying this combination leaves B as the correct answer. Answers A, C and D are therefore incorrect.

Road Policing, para. 3.1.2.2

Answer 1.7

Answer **D** — Under s. 108(1) of the Road Traffic Act 1988, 'medium-sized' goods vehicles are those constructed to carry or haul goods, which are not adapted to carry more than 9 passengers, *including* the driver.

The maximum permissible weight of such a vehicle will exceed 3.5 tonnes.

Answer D is the only option that covers accurately both points and therefore answers A, B and C are incorrect.

Road Policing, para. 3.1.2.3

Answer 1.8

Answer **C** — Under s. 108(1) of the Road Traffic Act 1988, the definition of a 'moped' is divided between those that were first used before 1 August 1977, and those first used on or after this date. Early mopeds (i.e. those in the first group) had to have pedals fitted, with an engine size not exceeding 50 cc. There was no restriction on speed. Answer B is therefore incorrect because pedals were not required on mopeds first used after the relevant date.

Mopeds which fall into the newer category are required to have a maximum design speed of 50 kilometres per hour and an engine size not exceeding 50 cc.

Answers A and D are a mixture of the definition of a moped, and the definition of a 'Learner Motor Bicycle' (which must *either* be propelled by electric power *or* have an engine size not exceeding 125 cc) and are therefore incorrect.

Road Policing, para. 3.1.2.4

Answer 1.9

Answer **A** — Under s. 121 of the Road Traffic Act 1988, a large passenger-carrying vehicle (PCV) is one which is constructed or adapted for carrying more than 16 passengers.

The definition does not mention the weight of the vehicle. In fact, the weight of 3.5 tonnes applies to the weight of *medium-sized goods* vehicles, which are constructed or adapted to haul goods, are of a permissible maximum weight which exceeds 3.5 but not 7.5 tonnes, and are not adapted to carry more than 9 passengers, including the driver (see s. 108(1)(c). Answer B is therefore incorrect.

If a vehicle is designed to carry more than 16 passengers, it will be classed as a large PCV, *regardless* of whether they are being carried for hire or reward. This condition applies to a small PCV, (which is constructed or adapted to carry more than 8 but not more than 16 passengers). Answer C is incorrect.

Finally, the 16 passengers *do not* include the driver of a large PCV; therefore, answer D is incorrect.

Road Policing, para. 3.1.2.6

Answer 1.10

Answer **A** — The general test which a court will apply is whether an *ordinary person* (not a reasonable person) would say that there had been an accident in all the circumstances. Answer D is therefore incorrect. It is immaterial what the driver of the vehicle thought at the time, and answer C is incorrect.

The term 'accident' *will* include a deliberate act committed by the driver of a vehicle, such as ramming a gate (*Chief Constable of Staffordshire* v *Lees* [1981] RTR 506). Consequently, answer B is incorrect.

Road Policing, para. 3.1.3.2

Answer 1.11

Answer **B** — It is possible for more than one person to be the 'driver' of a vehicle as s. 192(1) of the Road Traffic Act 1988 makes provision for the 'steersman' to be a 'driver'. This was confirmed in the case of *Tyler* v *Whatmore* [1976] RTR 83, when one person was sitting in the driver's seat and the other leaned across and operated the steering wheel. Answer A is therefore incorrect.

The only situation where the above rule does not apply is in a case of causing death by dangerous driving under s. 1 of the 1988 Act. Answer C is incorrect, as the rule *will* apply in the case of dangerous driving.

Answer D is incorrect because the rule does allow for both to be charged, subject to the exception above.

Road Policing, para. 3.1.3.3

Answer 1.12

Answer **B** — For the purposes of road traffic offences, a person who takes out a vehicle remains the 'driver' of it until he or she has completed that journey. Therefore, even if the vehicle is stationary for some time, the person may still be the 'driver' if he or she has not completed the journey (see *Jones* v *Prothero* [1952] 1 All

ER 434) (answer A is incorrect). Answer D is incorrect as this period could be for some time. The fact that the person had not set the handbrake, or was using the brake, is not relevant in this context, as the offence would still be made out if the handbrake was set. However, this evidence would probably assist in any prosecution. Answer C is therefore incorrect.

Road Policing, para. 3.1.3.3

Answer 1.13

Answer **D** — There are many different cases ruling on whether or not a person is 'driving' a vehicle. This is because the question is one of *fact* and courts are largely left to decide each on its own merits. Mere suspicion on the part of the arresting or reporting officer will not be sufficient to prove this aspect of the relevant offence (see *R (on the application of Huntley)* v *DPP* [2004] EWHC 870). This question will be decided by considering the extent to which the person has control of both the direction and movement of the vehicle.

The cases covered by the question offer helpful guidance. In *R* v *MacDonagh* [1974] RTR 372, the defendant was pushing his car, while leaning through the window to steer it. He was held *not* to be 'driving'; answer A is therefore incorrect. The person *was* 'driving' in *Gunnell* v *DPP* [1994] RTR 151, where the person was sitting astride his motorbike and was pushing it along with both feet. However in option B with no forward momentum or engine running, this would not fit the definition as given above. Answer B is therefore incorrect. In *Jones* v *Pratt* [1983] RTR 54, the person was *not* driving when he was the front seat passenger in a car and grabbed the steering wheel suddenly, to stop the driver hitting an animal. Answer C is therefore incorrect. Contrast *Jones* v *Pratt* with *Tyler* v *Whatmore* in Answer 1.11. The main difference between the two cases would appear to be that in the latter case, Tyler was in control for a little while, whereas in the former, Jones was in control only momentarily.

Recently the Divisional Court has accepted a finding that operating the controls of a car stuck on a grass verge with the wheels spinning but with no movement of the vehicle was 'driving' (*DPP* v *Alderton* [2003] EWHC 2917).

Road Policing, para. 3.1.3.4

Answer 1.14

Answer **D** — Acts which are merely preparatory will not amount to attempting to drive. Merely sitting in a car would not be sufficient, as this is still a preparatory act. Answer C is therefore incorrect.

It has been held that, where a defendant sits in the driver's seat of a car and tries to put his or her house keys in the ignition, that behaviour may be enough to prove a charge of 'attempting to drive' (*Kelly* v *Hogan* [1982] RTR 352). Answer A is therefore incorrect.

The fact that the vehicle is incapable of being driven will not prevent a charge involving an 'attempt' to drive (*R* v *Farrance* [1978] RTR 225). Answer B is incorrect because the question asks for the *first* point at which the defendant could be guilty of 'attempting' to drive.

Road Policing, para. 3.1.3.5

Answer 1.15

Answer **A** — The case of *DPP* v *Watkins* [1989] 2 WLR 966 outlines the principles to be applied when considering whether or not a person is 'in charge' of a vehicle.

Where the defendant is the owner of the vehicle, *or* where he or she has recently driven it, it will be for him or her to show that there was no likelihood of his or her resuming control while he or she was drunk.

Where the defendant is not the owner, or has not recently driven the vehicle, the prosecution will only need to show that the defendant was in voluntary control of the vehicle, or intended to become so in the immediate future. Answers B and D are incorrect for this reason.

Answer C is incorrect, as the defendant must show that it is *unlikely* that he will drive while unfit, not that he had no *intention* of doing so — a slight difference in wording, but nevertheless important in the context of the case.

Road Policing, para. 3.1.3.6

Answer 1.16

Answer **B** — The 'keeper' of a vehicle can be a different person to the 'owner'. Whereas the 'owner' of the vehicle will remain so until he or she disposes of the vehicle, the 'keeper' can cease to be so if he or she temporarily parts with the vehicle (*R* v *Parking Adjudicator, ex parte The Mayor and Burgesses of the London Borough Council of Wandsworth*, The Times, 22 July 1996).

Therefore, while HILTON has not transferred ownership of the vehicle, he is no longer the 'keeper', albeit on a temporary basis. Answers A and D are therefore incorrect.

Section 62(2) of the Vehicle Excise and Registration Act 1994 states that a person 'keeps' the vehicle if he or she causes it to be on a road for any period, however short, when it is not in use there. Therefore, answer C is incorrect.

Road Policing, para. 3.1.3.7

Answer 1.17

Answer **C** — When a person's movements are beyond his or her control, or his or her actions are involuntary, he or she will not generally be liable in criminal law as the element of *actus reus* is not present. It is also highly likely that because there is no willed action or omission by the defendant, he or she will not have the required state of mind (*mens rea*). A defence is provided in such circumstances, namely 'automatism'. Answers A and D are therefore incorrect.

There is no automatic defence of *automatism;* it will be available only in certain circumstances (answer B is therefore incorrect). If a person has a particular medical condition, which is likely to occur when he or she is driving, he or she has a duty to take reasonable steps to avoid driving when the symptoms are likely to arise (*R* v *Sibbles* [1959] Crim LR 660). This case is supported by *Moses* v *Winder* [1981] RTR 37 (which relates specifically to a diabetic undergoing a hypoglycaemic attack).

Road Policing, para. 3.1.3.8

Answer 1.18

Answer **A** — A road is defined under s. 192(1) of the Road Traffic Act 1988 as:

(a) in relation to England and Wales,

> ... any highway and any other road to which the public has access, and includes bridges over which a road passes,

This definition (or one very similar to it, e.g. under s. 142(1) of the Road Traffic Regulation Act 1984) is applicable to most occasions where the expression 'road' is used in statutes.

If a vehicle is partly on the road and partly on some other privately owned land, it can be treated as being on a 'road' for the purposes of road traffic legislation (*Randall* v *Motor Insurers' Bureau* [1969] 1 All ER 21).

Whether the public has access is a question of fact. If only a restricted section of the public (such as members of a club) has access to a road, that is not enough to make it a 'road' (*Blackmore* v *Chief Constable of Devon and Cornwall*, The Times, 6 December 1984). Answer B is therefore incorrect.

Any access enjoyed by the public must be with the agreement of the landowner. As Lord Sands put it in *Blackmore*, the members of the public must not have obtained access 'either by overcoming a physical obstruction or in defiance of prohibition, express or implied'. Therefore roads are capable of being closed or cordoned off in a way that alters their status as such. Answers C and D are therefore incorrect.

Don't get confused, as the courts sometimes do, with what is a 'public place' as opposed to a road. A good example is where the defendant collided with a caravan on a campsite and was charged with driving on a 'road' whilst over the prescribed limit. The Divisional Court held that the magistrates had given too much consideration to the public access point and not enough to the overall question as to whether the location amounted to a 'road' (*R (on the application of Dunmill)* v *DPP* [2004] EWHC 1700)

Road Policing, para. 3.1.3.9

Answer 1.19

Answer **C** — The situation regarding car parks becoming roads was reviewed as a result of two cases, namely, *Clarke* v *Kato* and *Cutter* v *Eagle Star Insurance Co. Ltd* [1998] 1 WLR 1647. Both of these cases were reviewed on appeal in the House of Lords, where the plaintiffs argued that there was no justification in extending the definition of a 'road' under the Road Traffic Act 1988. The car park in each case was provided solely for parking vehicles. Their Lordships held that whether a particular location falls within the definition of a road under the Act will ultimately be one of fact for the courts to decide. Also, that it would only be in exceptional circumstances that a car park could fall within the definition of a road. The court further held that the parking bays within a car park *could not* be regarded as an integral part of the highway, leading into the car park. Consequently, answers A, B and D are incorrect.

Road Policing, para. 3.1.3.9

Answer 1.20

Answer **A** — In order for a place to be a 'public place', it must be shown by the prosecution that:

- the people admitted to the place are members of the public and are admitted for that reason, and not because they belong to a certain or special class of the public; *and*
- those people are so admitted with the permission, express or implied, of the owner of the land.

(*DPP* v *Vivier* [1991] RTR 205).

The above case shows that the place in question must be open to *all* members of the public, without restriction (answer B is therefore incorrect). It is irrelevant whether the people are there with permission if only restricted members of the public are present. The two requirements from the *Vivier* case go hand in hand and answer C is therefore incorrect.

The fact that people had to pay to enter the land is completely irrelevant as to whether it is a public place. It is the *class of people* that are allowed entry (or not) that is important. If the fête had been open to *all* members of the public and they had all been made to pay, it would have been a public place. (Answer D is therefore incorrect.)

Road Policing, para. 3.1.3.10

Answer 1.21

Answer **A** — The circumstances in the question mirror those in the case of *R* v *DPP, ex parte Taussik* [2001] ACD 10. In this case, the Divisional Court took the view that the evidence provided by the police was very thin, and that they had not shown that motorists other than residents used the access road regularly. This meant that the court could not find that the road was a public place. The court held that such a road *could* become a public place (therefore answers B and D are incorrect), but it was essential that the prosecution provided *clear* evidence that the road was used by motorists other than residents and that they should present factual details of who used the road and for what purpose. Answer C is incorrect for this reason.

Road Policing, para. 3.1.3.10

Answer 1.22

Answer **C** — In order to prove that a place is in fact a 'public place' for the purposes of road traffic offences, it must be shown by the prosecution that:

- those people who are admitted to the place in question are members of the public and are admitted as such, not as members of some special or particular class of the public (e.g. people belonging to an exclusive club) or as a result of some special characteristic that is not shared by the public at large; *and*
- those people are so admitted with the permission, express or implied, of the owner of the land in question.

(*DPP* v *Vivier* [1991] RTR 205).

Customers for this pub are members of the general public who are invited to use it by the licensee, therefore making it public and not a 'special class' of persons e.g. members of a club, and therefore answers B and D are incorrect.

The importance of police officers providing enough evidence to show that a particular location amounted to a public place was highlighted in *R* v *DPP, ex parte Taussik* [2001] ACD 10. In that case the defendant was stopped as she drove out of an access road leading from a block of flats. The road was a cul-de-sac leading off a highway and was maintained by the local housing department. At the entrance to it there was large sign saying 'Private Residents Only'. As there was no evidence from the officers themselves that they had seen motorists (other than residents) using the road, the court was unable to conclude that the road was anything other than a private one. Contrast this with *R (on the application of Lewis)* v *DPP* [2004] EWHC 3081 where the court held it was not necessary for the prosecution to adduce evidence that a pub car park was a public place, given that it was attached to the public house and given a general invitation to use it by the licensee. Therefore answer A is incorrect.

Road Policing, para. 3.1.3.10

Answer 1.23

Answer **D** — A road is defined under s. 192(1) of the Road Traffic Act 1988 as:

(a) in relation to England and Wales,

> . . . any highway and any other road to which the public has access, and includes bridges over which a road passes,

A 'highway' is a way over which the public has a right to pass and re-pass by foot, horse or vehicle, or with animals (*Lang* v *Hindhaugh* [1986] RTR 271). For a highway to exist, there must be some form of 'dedication' of the relevant land to the public and, once so dedicated, it is unlikely that the public status of a highway can be changed.

Unlike a road, a highway does not cease to be such when it is temporarily roped off or closed (*McCrone* v *J & L Rigby (Wigan) Ltd* (1950) 50 LGR 115).

Highways will include public bridleways and footways; they also include public bridges over which they pass. Broadly, footways are the bits of a highway that you walk on and carriageways are the bits that you drive on. Bridleways, as the name suggests, are highways where the public have a right to ride or lead horses (and related animals), or to pass on foot. Therefore, logically, if a 'bridleway' is a 'highway', and a 'highway' is a 'road', then a 'bridleway' is also a 'road'. Answers A, B and C are therefore incorrect.

Road Policing, para. 3.1.3.11

Answer 1.24

Answer **D** — Offences relating to 'using' a vehicle are generally committed by the driver and the driver's employer. For the employer to commit the offence of 'using', the person driving the vehicle must be doing so in the ordinary course of his or her employer's business (*West Yorkshire Trading Standards Service* v *Lex Vehicle Leasing Ltd* [1996] RTR 70). It must be proved that:

- the employer owned the vehicle;
- the driver was employed by the employer; *and*
- the driver was driving in the ordinary course of his or her employment

(*Jones* v *DPP* [1999) RTR 1).

It is immaterial that the employer has not specifically authorised the employee to use the vehicle in such a way (*Richardson* v *Baker* [1976] RTR 56). Answers A and B are therefore incorrect.

The owner of a trailer who is responsible for putting it on a road will not escape liability by arguing that it was being drawn and therefore 'used' by someone else (*Forwarding Ltd* v *DPP* [1989] RTR 239).

Answer C is therefore incorrect.

Road Policing, para. 3.1.3.13

Answer 1.25

Answer **D** — If a vehicle is shown to be a 'motor vehicle' and it is on a road, it may be said to be in 'use', even if it is in such a state that it cannot be driven (*Pumbien* v *Vines* [1996] RTR 37). Therefore answer A is incorrect.

It is generally the case that a passenger in a car does not 'use' the vehicle. However, if a passenger arranges to travel in or on a vehicle for his or her benefit, he or she will 'use' the vehicle (*Cobb* v *Williams* [1973] RTR 113). A passenger can also 'use' a vehicle if there is an element of 'joint enterprise' (*O'Mahoney* v *Jollife and Motor Insurers' Bureau* [1999] RTR 245). Answer B is therefore incorrect.

The Divisional Court has applied a broader interpretation to the meaning of 'use' when considering offences involving trailers. The court held that the owner of a defective trailer who is responsible for putting it on a road should not be able to escape liability for its condition simply by arguing that it was being drawn — and therefore 'used' by someone else (*NFC Forwarding Ltd* v *DPP* [1989] RTR 239). Therefore answer C is incorrect.

If a person driving a vehicle is doing so in the ordinary course of his or her employer's business, the employer is using the vehicle (see e.g. *West Yorkshire Trading Standards Service* v *Lex Vehicle Leasing Ltd* [1996] RTR 70). In such a case you must prove that:

- the defendant (employer) actually owned the vehicle;
- at the relevant time, the driver was employed by the defendant; and
- the driver was driving the vehicle in the ordinary course of his or her employment

(*Jones* v *DPP* [1999] RTR 1).

If the driver is not an employee then the employer is not using the vehicle, even if that driver is a partner of the firm or has been asked to drive the vehicle by the employer (*Crawford* v *Haughton* [1972] 1 WLR 572).

Road Policing, para. 3.1.3.13

Answer 1.26

Answer **B** — 'Causing' will involve some degree of dominance or control, or express mandate from the 'causer'.

Causing requires both positive action and knowledge by the defendant (*Price* v *Cromack* [1975] 1 WLR 988). Therefore it is not enough that the person in charge is aware an offence is being committed; he or she must have done something to contribute to it. Neither person in the scenario could meet these criteria, as neither 'ordered' the offences to be committed (one person was unaware of what was going on).

Further, wilful blindness by employers to their employees' unlawful actions is not enough to amount to 'causing' the offence, (*Redhead Freight Ltd* v *Shulman* (1989) RTR 1). Answers A, C and D are incorrect for these reasons.

Road Policing, para. 3.1.3.15

Answer 1.27

Answer **D** — Generally in order to prove a case of 'permitting' there must be proof of knowledge by the defendant of the vehicle's use *and* of the unlawful nature of that use. In other words, there must be proof that the defendant knew the vehicle was being used and that the driver was committing an offence by using it. Answers A, B and C are incorrect for this reason.

Road Policing, para. 3.1.3.16

2 Offences Involving Standards of Driving

STUDY PREPARATION

Offences involving standards of driving are among the most frequently encountered of road traffic offences. The key to understanding such offences — and any relevant defences — lies in knowing:

- the classification of vehicle covered by the offence;
- the *place* in which the offence can be committed; *and*
- the mental element required.

It should be noted that there is only one standard of driving that is acceptable of any driver, irrespective of his or her particular driving experience or qualifications.

It is also worth noting the application of road traffic law to police drivers and those from other emergency services.

Under the Police Reform Act 2002, police officers and police community support officers (PCSOs) are given additional powers to deal with drivers who use vehicles to cause harassment to members of the public. Finally, the much publicised law relating to the use of hand-held mobile phones was introduced in December 2003, and receives attention in this chapter.

QUESTIONS

Question 2.1

Section 1 of the Road Traffic Act 1988 relates to the offence of causing death by dangerous driving.

Which statement below most accurately describes where this offence may be committed, and in which type of vehicle?

A Motor vehicle, on a road only.
B Mechanically propelled vehicle, on a road or public place.
C Motor vehicle, on a road or public place.
D Mechanically propelled vehicle, on a road only.

Question 2.2

HENNIGAN was driving a stolen vehicle and WEBB was a passenger. They were driving at 60 mph, approaching a junction, when HENNIGAN told WEBB to pull the handbrake up. He tried to do a handbrake turn, but lost control when WEBB pulled the handbrake, and collided with a wall. WEBB was killed in the accident, but HENNIGAN survived.

Would HENNIGAN be guilty of causing the death of WEBB by dangerous driving in these circumstances?

A Yes, if it can be shown he was a substantial cause of WEBB's death.
B No, as WEBB contributed substantially to his own death.
C Yes, if it can be shown he was the sole cause of WEBB's death.
D Yes, if it can be shown he contributed in some way to WEBB's death.

Question 2.3

DALEY was driving her car on the approach to a zebra crossing when some children were crossing the road. When DALEY applied her brakes, they failed and she knocked over a child, injuring her. DALEY's car was examined and it was found that her brake discs were worn so much that they did not work. DALEY stated that she had heard the brakes squealing earlier in her journey, but had not realised how bad they were.

What further evidence, if any, would be required in order to convict DALEY of driving dangerously?

A That it would have been obvious to a competent and careful driver that driving the vehicle in that condition would be dangerous.
B No further evidence is required; DALEY may be convicted on these facts alone.
C DALEY could not be convicted of dangerous driving, as she was unaware of the dangerous condition of her car.
D That it should have been obvious to DALEY that driving the vehicle in that condition would be dangerous.

Question 2.4

NEWMAN was involved in an accident where he drove into the wall of a house, situated on a sharp bend. Nobody was injured in the accident, but substantial damage was caused to the house. There were no witnesses to the accident itself. However, GORDON told the police that NEWMAN had overtaken her before the bend and, in her opinion, he was driving too fast.

What evidence would GORDON be able to give, in order to support a prosecution against NEWMAN for dangerous driving?

A None, as no people suffered injury or death as a direct result of the accident.
B That the vehicle was driven below the standards expected of a competent and careful driver, prior to the accident.
C None, as GORDON was not a witness to the accident itself, her evidence amounts to 'hearsay' evidence.
D That the vehicle was driven far below the standards expected of a competent and careful driver, prior to the accident.

Question 2.5

HEWITT has been charged with an offence of dangerous driving, under s. 2A of the Road Traffic Act 1988. The prosecution intends to introduce evidence of the presence of a Class A drug in HEWITT's blood when the offence was committed.

Would the evidence of the Class A drug be relevant to whether or not HEWITT drove dangerously?

A Yes, provided it can be shown the quantity of the drug was sufficient to adversely affect HEWITT's driving.
B Yes, the presence of the controlled drug alone would be relevant to this offence.
C No, evidence that a person had a controlled drug in their blood would not be relevant to this offence.
D Yes, provided it can be shown there was a direct link between the presence of the drug and HEWITT's driving.

Question 2.6

HIGGINSON has been charged with causing death by dangerous driving in relation to a road traffic collision.

In relation to the actual causes of the collision, which of the following is true?

A Any police officer may give an opinion, but it *must* be supported with factual evidence.

B A police officer who has experience in collision investigation may give such opinion.

C A police officer who has experience in collision investigation may give such opinion but it *must* be supported with factual evidence.

D Only factual evidence in relation to the dangerous driving is allowed. Opinion as to the cause of the collision is not.

Question 2.7

O'BRIEN has been convicted of an offence of dangerous driving and is awaiting sentence by the court.

In relation to disqualification and having to take an extended driving test (re-test) which of the following is true?

A O'BRIEN must be disqualified and discretionary re-test.

B O'BRIEN must be disqualified and compulsory re-test.

C O'BRIEN should be disqualified unless special reasons exist, if disqualified discretionary re-test.

D O'BRIEN should be disqualified unless special reasons exist, if disqualified compulsory re-test.

Question 2.8

A team from the local rugby club has entered a charity bike ride. The machine they are riding is pedal powered and has 6 seats and 2 wheels. During practice, and as a joke, they decide to ride it through the local town centre, in the pedestrianised area. They ride faster and faster, narrowly missing pedestrians, until they knock over a lady and her child causing them both injuries.

Which of the following is true?

A This could be dangerous, careless and inconsiderate cycling even though it was not on a road.

B This could be dangerous, careless and inconsiderate cycling or wanton or furious driving even though it was not on a road.

C This could only be wanton or furious driving as it was in a public place and not on a road.

D This could be neither dangerous, careless and inconsiderate cycling or wanton or furious driving as it was not on a road.

Question 2.9

McCRONE was involved in a road traffic accident when he drove into a parked car, having lost concentration momentarily. At the time of the accident, McCRONE was learning to drive in a driving school car and was accompanied by RIDING, his driving instructor.

In relation to McCRONE's state of mind, what would the prosecution need to prove in order to convict him of driving without due care and attention?

A Either that McCRONE knew, or was aware of the fact that his driving fell far below the required standard.

B The prosecution have nothing to prove in relation to McCRONE's state of mind, there is no statutory defence.

C That McCRONE was aware of the fact that his driving fell below the required standard.

D The prosecution have nothing to prove in relation to McCRONE's state of mind, but he may have a statutory defence due to his inexperience.

Question 2.10

PARSONS is appearing before the court on a count of careless driving contrary to s. 3 of the Road Traffic Act 1988. PARSONS claims that he ran into the back of the car in front because children playing by the roadside distracted him.

The court, however, may find that the distraction will not absolve PARSONS of the consequences of not paying attention. Which of the following will *not* be a factor affecting the distraction that the court may consider relevant?

A How long the driver was distracted for.

B The speed the vehicle was travelling at.

C Any other hazards on the road at that time.

D How experienced the driver was.

Question 2.11

DILKS was driving his car in the open-air car park of a large shopping centre, on a busy Saturday. It was raining heavily and DILKS decided to soak some pedestrians by driving through puddles. The first group he picked on were standing in a bus shelter. DILKS drove past and sprayed water on the shelter window and nobody got wet. The second group was not protected and several people were soaked as a result of his actions.

Has DILKS committed an offence under s. 3 of the Road Traffic Act 1988, by driving without due consideration?

A Yes, but only in relation to the second group of pedestrians.

B No, as no other drivers were affected by his actions.

C Yes, in relation to both groups of pedestrians.

D No, as the incidents did not take place on a road.

Question 2.12

MUNDIE was driving his car along a country road when, as he was approaching a bend, he crossed the central white line dividing the two lanes. As he crossed the line, he nearly collided with another vehicle.

Would the evidence that MUNDIE crossed the white line be conclusive proof alone of driving without due care and attention, contrary to s. 3 of the Road Traffic Act 1988?

A No, MUNDIE would need to have committed at least one other driving error.

B Yes, depending on MUNDIE's explanation of what happened.

C Yes, no further proof would be required to prove the offence.

D No, a single driving error will not amount to an offence under this section.

Question 2.13

DEERE retired from work and went on a touring holiday to Europe for six months. DEERE's teenage son, JEFFREY, was allowed to use the family car while DEERE was away. In the first month, the car was seized from JEFFREY for using it while causing harassment. Several times during the following months, the relevant authority wrote to DEERE, the registered owner, serving notice that the vehicle had been seized. Upon returning from holiday, DEERE discovered that JEFFREY had ignored all correspondence from the authority and that as no reply had been received, the vehicle had been sold at a car auction.

Would DEERE have the right to claim the proceeds from the sale of the vehicle?

A No, the proceeds may be kept by the authority, as DEERE failed to comply with the seizure notice.

B Yes, DEERE can claim the net proceeds from the sale in these circumstances alone.

C No, unless it can be shown that the authority did not take reasonable steps to contact DEERE before the vehicle was sold.

D Yes, provided it can be shown that DEERE was not aware the vehicle would be driven in such a manner by JEFFREY.

Question 2.14

PEARCE is a designated police community support officer (PCSO) working on a housing estate. He has received a number of complaints from residents about HOGAN riding his motor cycle in a park nearby. Last week, PEARCE stopped HOGAN while he was riding his motor cycle and issued him with a warning under s. 59 of the Police Reform Act 2002, as he had narrowly missed colliding with some children playing football. PEARCE has today received a further complaint about HOGAN, who again rode his motor cycle in the park, nearly injuring a child. PEARCE attended HOGAN's home address and saw the motor cycle on the road outside.

Does PEARCE have the power to seize HOGAN's motor cycle, under s. 59(3)(b) of the Police Reform Act 2002, in these circumstances?

A No, a PCSO's power is restricted to stopping vehicles.

B Yes, he has the power to seize and remove the vehicle in these circumstances.

C Yes, provided he is accompanied by a police officer in uniform.

D No, as the motor cycle is no longer being used.

Question 2.15

GATES was driving a car on the approach to a pelican crossing — the lights were showing red. TODD stepped into the road on the crossing; however, GATES was distracted at the time and collided with TODD. GATES drove off without stopping. TODD was taken to hospital, but died 10 hours after the collision. GATES attended the police station 24 hours after the collision, and provided a negative sample during a procedure under s. 7 of the Road Traffic Act 1988.

Given that GATES was guilty of driving without due care and attention, were the police correct in requesting a breath sample in these circumstances (consider legislation under s. 3A(1) of the Road Traffic Act 1988)?

A No, the request for the sample was not made within 18 hours of the accident.

B Yes, the request for a *screening test* must take place within 18 hours of the accident; it is not relevant when the request is made under s.7.

C Yes, request for the sample took place within 18 hours of TODD's death.

D Yes, the length of time between the collision and the breath sample is irrelevant in these circumstances.

Question 2.16

CAGE works for a building company and has a drug habit. CAGE turned up for work whilst under the influence of drugs and was fired. To get revenge, CAGE stole a dumper truck from the site, intending to take it to the head office and cause damage. On the way, CAGE was involved in a road traffic collision, whereby a pedestrian walked into the road in front of the dumper truck, and was killed. CAGE was still under the influence of drugs at this time.

Has CAGE committed an offence under s. 3A of the Road Traffic Act 1988, in these circumstances?

A No, CAGE was not under the influence of drink at the time of the accident.

B No, it must be shown that CAGE drove without due care and attention or without due consideration to other road users.

C No, he was not driving a motor vehicle at the time of the accident.

D Yes, he was driving a mechanically propelled vehicle on a road whilst under the influence of drugs.

Question 2.17

Section 38(7) of the Road Traffic Act 1988 refers to the use of the Highway Code in court proceedings.

In relation to s. 38, which of the following statements is correct?

A A failure by a person to observe a provision of the Highway Code may be used *only* in civil proceedings, to establish any liability as to their driving.

B The stopping distances shown in the Highway Code are admissible in speeding cases in court, although not definitive proof of speeding.

C A failure by a person to observe a provision of the Highway Code may be used in criminal or civil proceedings, to establish *or* negate any liability as to their driving.

D A failure by a person to observe a provision of the Highway Code may be used in criminal or civil proceedings, to establish *only* their liability as to their driving.

Question 2.18

YOUNG was a passenger in a motor vehicle that was travelling along a busy dual carriageway. At this time, he was supervising GLOVER, a learner driver. YOUNG received a text message on his mobile phone from his wife, telling him he had to pick up his children from school. At this time, it was not practicable to pull over due to the nature of the road; therefore, YOUNG sent a text message to his wife saying that he would do so. YOUNG was not using a hands-free device at this time.

Who, if either, would commit an offence because of YOUNG's use of a mobile phone in these circumstances?

A YOUNG for using the phone and GLOVER for permitting its use.

B Only YOUNG commits the offence in these circumstances.

C Neither, as it was not practicable for GLOVER to stop in the circumstances.

D Neither, as YOUNG did not make a telephone call.

Question 2.19

Constable PIERCE was dealing with a road traffic accident, which involved serious injuries to one driver. The driver of the other vehicle left the scene without stopping. A Police National Computer (PNC) check revealed that the registered keeper of the vehicle, LOWE, lived nearby. Constable PIERCE attended LOWE's address immediately to ascertain who was driving the vehicle.

What does s. 172 of the Road Traffic Act 1988 say in relation to Constable PIERCE's ability to ascertain these details?

A A request may be made verbally by Constable PIERCE, and LOWE has 28 days in which to reply.

B A request may only be made by post, and LOWE would have 28 days in which to reply.

C A request may be made verbally by Constable PIERCE, and LOWE must reply immediately.

D Constable PIERCE may not make the request, this power is restricted to people authorised by the Chief Officer of Police.

Question 2.20

YORKE was issued with a provisional Fixed Penalty Notice (FPN) for speeding and was sent a document under s. 172 of the Road Traffic Act 1988, requesting details of the driver. When YORKE replied to the notice, he sent a signed letter to the prosecuting authorities admitting he was the driver. However, he did *not* fill out the document issued under s. 172, and returned the unsigned form with his letter. Later, during a court hearing, YORKE pleaded not guilty, claiming that because he had not signed the document issued under s. 172, he had not made a 'statement' under s. 12 of the Road Traffic Offenders Act 1988, and therefore his admission was not admissible.

Is YORKE's defence likely to succeed in these circumstances?

A No, if the police can show that YORKE deliberately attempted to avoid prosecution by his actions.

B Yes, because he did not complete the correct form, the police had a duty to re-serve the notice.

C Yes, because the form was not signed, the police had a duty to re-serve the notice.

D No, the police are entitled to require the person providing the information to sign the relevant form.

Question 2.21

The Divisional Court has ruled that the requirement to respond to a notice issued under s. 172 of the Road Traffic Act 1988 (providing details of the driver of a vehicle) does not infringe a person's right against self-incrimination.

What further advice did the Divisional Court offer, where the defendant disputes the reliability of an admission as to who was the driver following the service of a notice under s. 172?

A The court *must* exercise their discretion to exclude written evidence and order the prosecution to adduce oral evidence in relation to the notice.

B The court need not require the prosecution to adduce oral evidence in the case, provided it can be shown that the notice was served correctly.

C The prosecution has the discretion to exclude written evidence and to adduce oral evidence in relation to the notice.

D The court *ought to* exercise their discretion to exclude written evidence and order the prosecution to adduce oral evidence in relation to the notice.

Question 2.22

O'TOOLE was driving an ambulance to a serious injury road traffic accident. O'TOOLE had activated the siren and flashing lights and was approaching a junction controlled by traffic lights, which were showing red. O'TOOLE slowed down on her approach, but drove through the red light. KEYSE, a pedestrian, stepped off the pavement into the path of the vehicle and was struck by the ambulance, sustaining injuries as a result.

In relation to O'TOOLE's driving, which of the following statements is correct?

A Emergency service crews are entitled to pass through red lights, and O'TOOLE may rely on this exemption to defend her driving.
B O'TOOLE will not be liable for the injuries caused to KEYSE in these circumstances, as she warned the pedestrian of her approach.
C O'TOOLE may be guilty of driving without due care and attention, but may have a defence because of the serious nature of the accident she was attending.
D O'TOOLE will be liable for the injuries caused to KEYSE in these circumstances, even though she warned the pedestrian of her approach.

Question 2.23

Where roadside speeding cameras catch an emergency service vehicle, a protocol now exists between the Association of Chief Police Officers (ACPO), the government and others. There is an assumption made where such a vehicle has warning lights activated in relation to the driver being exempt from speeding offences.

What is that assumption?

A That the exemption does apply.
B That the exemption does apply, unless there is evidence to the contrary.
C That the exemption does not automatically apply where only lights are working.
D That the exemptions will not automatically apply, unless there is evidence to the contrary, i.e. a call log.

Question 2.24

MARTIN owed BELL a considerable amount of money. BELL threatened to set fire to MARTIN's car if the money was not paid immediately. MARTIN persuaded his brother to lend him the money and he drove to BELL's house. On his way, MARTIN was stopped by the police, who discovered he was a disqualified driver. MARTIN claimed he was acting under duress, and would not have driven had it not been for the threat made by BELL.

Would MARTIN be entitled to claim a defence of duress in these circumstances?

A No, the defence will apply only where death is threatened.
B No, the defence will apply only where death or serious injury are threatened.

C Yes, the defence will apply where serious damage has been threatened.

D No, the defence will not apply in a case of disqualified driving.

Question 2.25

JOHN and BARBARA were divorced and had a 12-year-old daughter who lived with BARBARA. JOHN was concerned for the welfare of his daughter as BARBARA had been displaying violent tendencies towards her. One evening, he was in the pub when he received a text message from his daughter, saying that BARBARA had threatened to harm her with a knife. JOHN drove to BARBARA's house despite the fact that he had consumed 6 pints of beer. He then drove his daughter to his mother's house, 5 miles away, and attended a local police station to report the incident. The officer receiving the report realised that JOHN had been drinking and requested a sample of breath. JOHN was later found to be over the limit and was charged with driving with excess alcohol.

Would JOHN be able to claim the defence of necessity, because of the circumstances leading to his arrest?

A Yes, because his daughter was at risk of serious harm.

B No, because it was his daughter that was at risk of serious harm and not JOHN himself.

C No, because of the distance JOHN drove after picking up his daughter.

D Yes, because his daughter was at risk of serious harm and the driving was not disproportionate to the harm threatened.

ANSWERS

Answer 2.1

Answer **B** — The offence of causing death by dangerous driving under s. 1 of the Road Traffic Act 1988 may be committed by a person driving a mechanically propelled vehicle on a road or public place. The Act gives a wide meaning to the types of vehicle that may commit the offence (including dumper trucks, cranes and quad bikes), and the location. Answers A, C and D are therefore incorrect.

Road Policing, para. 3.2.2

Answer 2.2

Answer **D** — To prove an offence under s. 1 of the Road Traffic Act 1988 (causing death by dangerous driving), it must be shown that a person other than the defendant died. The driving by the defendant must be shown to have been a cause of the death. It is not necessary to show that it was the sole or even a substantial cause of death (*R* v *Hennigan* [1971] 3 All ER 133). Answers A and C are therefore incorrect.

It is irrelevant whether or not the person killed contributed to the incident, which resulted in his or her death. Answer B is therefore incorrect.

Road Policing, para. 3.2.2.1

Answer 2.3

Answer **A** — Section 2A(2) of the Road Traffic Act 1988 states:

> (2) A person is also to be regarded as driving dangerously for the purposes of sections 1 and 2 above if it would be obvious to a competent and careful driver that driving the vehicle in its current state would be dangerous.

The test is an objective one which looks at the manner of driving and *not* at the defendant's state of mind. It must be proved that:

- the dangerous condition would itself have been obvious to a competent and careful driver; *or*
- the defendant actually *knew* of its condition

(*R* v *Strong* [1995] Crim LR 428).

Answer B is incorrect, as the prosecution has to prove one of the above requirements.

Answer C is incorrect for the same reason.

Answer D is incorrect as the dangerous driving must have been obvious to a competent and careful driver — not simply to DALEY herself.

However, see the case of *R* v *Marchant and Muntz* [2003] Crim LR 806, where the prosecution failed to convince the Court of Appeal that a vehicle was dangerous as a result of its being 'manufactured' in that way.

Road Policing, paras 3.2.2.2, 3.2.2.3

Answer 2.4

Answer **D** — For the purposes of s. 1 of the Road Traffic Act 1988, under s. 2A(1) of the Act a person is to be regarded as driving dangerously if:

(a) the way he drives falls *far* below what would be expected of a competent and careful driver; *and*

(b) it would be obvious to a competent and careful driver that driving in that way would be dangerous.

Answer B is incorrect, as the 'far' is missing.

Answer C is incorrect because evidence showing how a particular vehicle was being driven before the incident itself may be given in support of the charge of dangerous driving. GORDON's 'opinion' would be relevant, because of the wording of s. 2A(1)(b) above.

Under s. 2A(3) of the 1988 Act, 'dangerous' refers to danger either of injury to a person or of serious damage to property. Answer A is therefore incorrect.

Road Policing, para. 3.2.2.2

Answer 2.5

Answer **B** — In some circumstances, the condition of the driver will be relevant to an offence of dangerous driving, under s. 2A of the Road Traffic Act 1988. In *R* v *Pleydell* [2005] EWCA Crim 1447, it was held that the mere presence of a controlled drug (such as cocaine) in a driver's blood may of itself be relevant to the issue of whether a person drove dangerously, (answers A and C are incorrect). This would be the case even if there is no specific evidence as to the drug's effect on that person's driving (answer D is therefore incorrect).

It should be noted that in *R* v *Woodward* [1995] RTR 130 the courts held that evidence of drink will also be admissible in an offence of causing the death of another by dangerous driving (under s. 1 of the Act) where the quantity of it may have adversely affected the quality of the defendant's driving.

Road Policing, para. 3.2.2.2

Answer 2.6

Answer **B** — Whether a witness is properly qualified in the subject calling for expertise is a question for the court. Such competence or skill may stem from formal study or training, experience, or both.

In *R* v *Oakley* [1979] Crim LR 657, a police officer who had attended a course, passed an exam as a collision investigator, and attended more than 400 accidents was entitled to give expert evidence as to the cause of a collision. Answers A and D are therefore incorrect.

The investigation of road traffic collisions is a science that has professional qualifications attached to them, and mathematical calculations that would not look out of place on a rocket scientist's desk! Although it is likely that factual evidence is likely to be available, a police officer meeting the *Oakley* criteria may give purely an opinion of how the collision occurred. Answer C is therefore incorrect.

Road Policing, para. 3.2.3

Answer 2.7

Answer **B** — A conviction for dangerous driving is covered by s. 36 of the Road Traffic Offenders Act 1988.

> (1) Where this subsection applies to a person the court must order him to be disqualified until he passes the appropriate driving test...
>
> (5) 'appropriate driving test' means —
>
> (a) an extended driving test, where a person is convicted of an offence involving obligatory disqualification or is disqualified under section 35 of this Act...

Disqualification is compulsory; therefore answers C and D are incorrect. As can be seen this disqualification runs until an extended test has been passed; answer A is therefore incorrect.

Road Policing, para. 3.2.3

Answer 2.8

Answer **C** — Dangerous, careless and inconsiderate cycling are specific offences found under ss. 28 and 29 of the Road Traffic Act 1988, but can only be committed on a road. Answers A and B are therefore incorrect. They are analogous to those relating to motor vehicles under 1988 Act. 'Cycles' will include tricycles and any cycle having four or more wheels (s. 192 of the 1988 Act).

The Offences Against the Person Act 1861, s. 35 relates to an offence of 'wanton or furious driving'. However, unlike the cycling offence above, s. 35 applies whether or not the conduct takes place on a road (*R* v *Cooke* [1971] Crim LR 44). It also covers any kind of vehicle or carriage, including bicycles (*R* v *Parker* (1895) 59 JP 793); answer D is therefore incorrect.

Road Policing, paras 3.2.3, 3.2.6

Answer 2.9

Answer **B** — 'Due care and attention' is the standard of driving that would be expected from a reasonable, prudent and competent driver in all the attendant circumstances. Once the prosecution has proved that the defendant has departed from that standard, and that his or her actions were 'voluntary', the offence is complete. There is no requirement to prove any *knowledge* or *awareness* by the defendant that his or her driving fell below that standard (*R* v *Lawrence* [1981] RTR 217). Answers A and C are therefore incorrect. There is only one *objective* standard of driving, which is expected of *all* drivers — even learner drivers (*McCrone* v *Riding* [1938] 1 All ER 157). Answer D is therefore incorrect.

Road Policing, para. 3.2.4

Answer 2.10

Answer **D** — The Administrative Court has accepted that there will be a defence available to a charge of careless driving where the driver can show that for some reason they were distracted (*Plunkett* v *DPP* [2004] EWHC 1937). However each case will be considered on its merits by the courts and certain factors including the nature and extent of the distraction in question. Amongst these factors will be:

- how long the distraction was;
- the speed of the vehicle;
- any other hazards present.

This list is not exclusive, but one factor that will not appear is that of the driver's experience. There is one objective standard of driving which is expected of all drivers — even learner drivers (*McCrone* v *Riding* [1938] 1 All ER 157). Once you have proved that a defendant departed from that standard of driving, and that his or her actions were 'voluntary', then the offence is complete. There is no need to prove any knowledge or awareness by the defendant that their driving fell below that standard (*R* v *Lawrence* [1981] 1 All ER 974).

Consequently answers A, B and C are incorrect.

Road Policing, para. 3.2.4

Answer 2.11

Answer **A** — An offence is committed under s. 3 of the Road Traffic Act 1988 when a person drives a mechanically propelled vehicle on a road or public place, without due care and attention, or without due consideration for other persons using the road or public place. As the offence may be committed in a public place, answer D is incorrect.

Other persons using the road or public place can include pedestrians who are deliberately sprayed with water from a puddle or passengers in a vehicle (*Pawley* v *Wharldall* [1965] 2 All ER 757). Answer B is therefore incorrect.

It must be shown that some other person was inconvenienced by the defendant's actions (*Dilks* v *Bowman-Shaw* [1981] RTR 4). No people were affected in the first group, answer C is therefore incorrect.

Road Policing, para. 3.2.4.1

Answer 2.12

Answer **B** — Breaching certain road traffic regulations will not always provide conclusive proof of an offence of driving without due care and attention, pursuant to s. 3 of the Road Traffic Act 1988. However, crossing a central white line without explanation *has* been held as conclusive proof of the offence, (see *Mundi* v *Warwickshire Police* [2001] EWHC Admin 448). Consequently, answers A, C and D are incorrect.

Road Policing, para. 3.2.4.1

Answer 2.13

Answer **B** — The arrangements for the removal, retention, release and disposal of vehicles are contained in the Police (Retention and Disposal of Motor Vehicles)

Regulations 2002. They cover the seizure, retention and disposal of vehicles under s. 59 of the Police Reform Act 2002.

The Regulations provide that seizure notices must be served on the owner of a vehicle and where the authority is unable to serve a notice on the owner, or the person fails to remove the vehicle from its custody, it must take further steps to identify the owner. Where the person appearing to be the owner fails to comply with a seizure notice, or where the authority has not been able, having taken all reasonable steps, to give the seizure notice to a person, the relevant authority can (subject to specific time limits) dispose of the vehicle, (see reg. 7).

Under reg. 8, if the vehicle is sold, the owner can claim the net proceeds (i.e. minus the storage fees) provided the claim is made within a year. It is immaterial that the owner failed to comply with the seizure notice (answer A is incorrect). There is no requirement for the owner to show that the authority has failed to comply with the regulations before making such a claim, or to demonstrate that he/she was not aware of the use of the vehicle which resulted in it being seized. Answers C and D are therefore incorrect.

Road Policing, para. 3.2.4.2

Answer 2.14

Answer **B** — To exercise one of the powers under s. 59(3) of the Act, a constable in uniform must have reasonable grounds for believing that a motor vehicle is being used on any occasion in a manner which contravenes s. 3 or s. 34 of the Road Traffic Act 1988, (careless/inconsiderate driving and prohibition of off-road driving), and is causing/likely to cause alarm, distress or annoyance to members of the public (s. 59(1)). Under s. 59(2) of the Act, a constable may also exercise a power under s. 59(3) if he or she has reasonable grounds for believing a motor vehicle *has been* used in circumstances outlined above. Answer D is incorrect.

The powers listed under s. 59(3) enable a constable in uniform to stop motor vehicles in contravention of s. 59(1) or (2) above, to seize and remove motor vehicles, enter any premises (except a dwelling) and use reasonable force if necessary. A vehicle may only be seized if a warning has previously been issued to the user of the vehicle that it will be seized if the use continues or is repeated and it appears to the officer that the use *has* continued or been repeated after the warning. The power to stop, seize and remove vehicles can be conferred on a PCSO, but he or she may not enter premises unless accompanied and supervised by a constable in uniform. Answers A and C are therefore incorrect.

Road Policing, para. 3.2.4.2

Answer 2.15

Answer **D** — Under s. 3A(1) of the Road Traffic Act 1988, if a person causes the death of another person by driving a mechanically propelled vehicle on a road or other public place without due care and attention, or without reasonable consideration for other persons using the road or place, and —

(a) he is, at the time when he is driving, unfit to drive through drink or drugs, or

(b) he has consumed so much alcohol that the proportion of it in his breath, blood or urine at that time exceeds the prescribed limit, or

(b) he is, within 18 hours after that time, required to provide a specimen in pursuance of section 7 of this Act, but without reasonable excuse fails to provide it, he is guilty of an offence.

This offence is committed where the defendant has driven without due care and attention, or without reasonable consideration and *either* he or she is unfit to drive through drink or drugs or over the prescribed limit, *or* he or she without reasonable excuse fails to provide a specimen within the appropriate time. Section 3A does *not* specify a timescale for the police to request a sample — the time is only relevant where the defendant fails to provide it within 18 hours of the accident. Answer D is correct (and answers A, B and C are incorrect) as the police can request this sample at any time after the accident.

For the offence to be complete, the request must be made within 18 hours after the driving which caused the death and not after the death itself. In addition, the offence is committed if the defendant fails to supply a sample for analysis under s. 7 of the Act, not s. 6 (screening test). Had GATES failed to supply a sample within 18 hours of the accident, answers B and C would be incorrect for this reason also.

Road Policing, para. 3.2.7

Answer 2.16

Answer **B** — Under s. 3A(1) of the Road Traffic Act 1988, if a person causes the death of another person by driving a mechanically propelled vehicle on a road or other public place without due care and attention, or without reasonable consideration for other persons using the road or place, and —

(a) he is, at the time when he is driving, unfit to drive through drink or drugs, or

(b) he has consumed so much alcohol that the proportion of it in his breath, blood or urine at that time exceeds the prescribed limit, or

(b) he is, within 18 hours after that time, required to provide a specimen in pursuance of section 7 of this Act, but without reasonable excuse fails to provide it, he is guilty of an offence.

In the first instance, a person must have driven without due care and attention, or without reasonable consideration for other persons using the road or place, which is why answer B is correct, and answer D is incorrect.

The offence may be committed by a person driving a mechanically propelled vehicle on a road or other public place, therefore, answer C is incorrect.

Finally, the defendant may commit this offence if, at the time he or she is unfit to drive through drink or drugs, or over the limit due to drink. Answer A is incorrect.

Road Policing, para. 3.2.7

Answer 2.17

Answer **C** — Under s. 38(7) of the Road Traffic Act 1988, a failure by a person to observe a provision of the Highway Code may be used in civil proceedings *or* criminal cases to establish *or* negate any liability as to their driving. Note this extends to both civil and criminal proceedings, and is used to establish *or* negate liability. Answers A and D are therefore incorrect.

The stopping distances shown in the Highway Code are *not* admissible in proving speeding cases in court, as they amount to *hearsay* (*R* v *Chadwick* [1975] Crim LR 105). Therefore answer B is incorrect.

Road Policing, para. 3.2.10

Answer 2.18

Answer **B** — There are three specific offences which may be prosecuted under s. 42 of the Road Traffic Act 1988:

- driving a motor vehicle while using a hand-held mobile telephone;
- permitting another person to *drive* a motor vehicle while using a hand-held mobile telephone; *and*
- using a hand-held mobile telephone while supervising a learner driver.

The offence of permitting the use of such a device will normally be directed at employers who require or expect drivers to make or receive communications using a hand-held device when driving. Since YOUNG was not driving the vehicle, GLOVER will not be guilty of this offence and answer A is incorrect.

The offence will be committed under *any* of the above three subsections if the hand-held device is used either to make a telephone call *or* to *perform any other interactive communication function by transmitting and receiving data*, which will include sending a text message, fax, email or picture. Answer D is therefore incorrect.

Lastly, there is a specific defence to this offence, if the driver (or supervisor) can show that he or she was using the hand-held device to make an emergency call to the police, fire, ambulance or other emergency services, that he or she was acting in response to a genuine emergency *and* that it was impracticable to cease driving (or for the provisional licence holder to cease driving). All three of these circumstances must apply before the defence can be considered. Since YOUNG's telephone call was not an emergency, it is immaterial that it was not practicable to stop, and he would have no defence. Answer C is therefore incorrect.

Road Policing, para. 3.2.10.1

Answer 2.19

Answer **C** — Under s. 172(2) of the Road Traffic Act 1988, where the driver of a vehicle has committed an offence to which the section applies (this includes ss. 3 and 170 (accidents)), the keeper of the vehicle shall give information as to the identity of the driver as required by or on behalf of a chief officer of police.

There is no mention of a person having to be authorised to make such a request on behalf of the chief officer and therefore it can be assumed that as Constable PIERCE is acting in the course of his duties, he is acting on behalf of the chief officer. Answer D is therefore incorrect.

When a request is made by post, the keeper has 28 days in which to reply. The 1988 Act does not state that *all* requests must be made by post and answer B is therefore incorrect. On the contrary, the case of *Lowe* v *Lester* [1987] RTR 30 indicates that requests may be made verbally, and the information must be provided within a reasonable time, which may in the prevailing circumstances mean *immediately*. Therefore, answer A is incorrect.

Road Policing, para. 3.2.11

Answer 2.20

Answer **D** — When a person is issued with a notice under s. 172 of the Road Traffic Act 1988, in order to meet the requirements of s. 12 of the Road Traffic Offenders Act 1988 and face proceedings, he or she is required to sign the notice giving details of the driver of the vehicle at that time. The circumstances in the question were examined in a number of court cases. In *Jones* v *DPP* [2004] EWHC 236, the defendant provided written information to the prosecuting authorities, as opposed to completing the relevant form. The court held that it is enough that the person gives the relevant information in writing, and the defendant's conviction was upheld. Answer B is therefore incorrect.

In *Mawdesly and Yorke* v *Chief Constable of Cheshire Constabulary* [2004] 1 All ER 58, it was claimed that the defendant had provided the relevant information but had omitted to sign the notice served under s. 172. The court held that the conviction should be set aside. However, this evidential loophole was closed when the Divisional Court ruled that a chief officer is entitled to *require* the person providing the information to sign the relevant notice served under s. 172 (*Francis* v *DPP* [2004] EWHC Admin 591). Answer C is incorrect — there is no requirement for the police to re-serve the notice if either of the above circumstances occur; neither do the police have to prove that the person deliberately attempted to avoid prosecution so answer A is incorrect.

Road Policing, para. 3.2.11

Answer 2.21

Answer **D** — The Divisional Court for England and Wales has confirmed that an admission to being the driver of a particular vehicle given in response to a s. 172 requirement does not breach the defendant's privilege against self-incrimination under Art. 6 of the European Convention (*DPP* v *Wilson* [2001] EWHC 198).

The court went on to say that, where a defendant disputed the reliability of any such admission, a judge (or magistrate) *ought to* exercise their general discretion to exclude the written evidence and require the prosecution to adduce oral evidence which could then be tested by cross-examination. Because of this, answer B is incorrect, and since the advice to the court is discretionary, answer A is also incorrect. The above decision is directed at the court, as opposed to the prosecution, therefore, answer C is incorrect.

Road Policing, para. 3.2.11.1

Answer 2.22

Answer **B** — There is no special exemption for emergency drivers with regard to standards of driving (*R* v *O'Toole* (1971) 55 Cr App R 206), and they will be judged against the standards of care which apply to *all* drivers. There is an exemption which allows emergency drivers to pass through red lights under the Traffic Signs Regulations 2002 (SI 2002/3113), reg. 36(1)(b). However, this *does not* exempt emergency drivers from having to drive with due care and attention. Answer A is therefore incorrect.

Answer C is incorrect because of the case of *DPP* v *Harris* [1995] RTR 100, where the driver of a police surveillance vehicle following a suspect drove through a red light. The court held that even though the suspects were being followed to the scene of an armed robbery, the seriousness of the circumstances did not provide an exemption.

Answer D is incorrect (and consequently answer B is correct), because of the ruling in the case of *Keyse* v *Commissioner of the Metropolitan Police* [2001] EWHC Cir. 715. This was a case defended on behalf of a police driver, but would presumably apply to other emergency service drivers. The court held that the police driver, who was driving with the vehicle's visual and audible warning equipment in operation, was not liable for the injuries to a pedestrian who stepped off the pavement into the path of the vehicle.

Road Policing, para. 3.2.12

Answer 2.23

Answer **B** — The protocol has been drawn up to reduce the bureaucratic burden on emergency service vehicles caused by roadside cameras. The assumption is that if the warning lights are activated then the exemption from speeding offences is applied to that vehicle as it is assumed in these circumstances that it is being used for its proper purpose. Answer C is therefore incorrect. This is not carte blanche immunity, as if there is evidence to the contrary the exemption will not automatically apply, for example if they were seen putting lights on immediately prior to the camera, and switching them off having passed the camera. Answer A is therefore incorrect.

That said, without such evidence to the contrary it is assumed the exemption applies and no further documentary evidence of proper usage of the vehicle is required; answer D is therefore incorrect.

Road Policing, para. 3.2.12

Answer 2.24

Answer **B** — The defence(s) of duress and necessity will apply to cases of dangerous driving, careless and inconsiderate driving *and* driving while disqualified (*R* v

Martin [1989] RTR 63 and *R* v *Backshall* [1998] 1 WLR 1506). Answer D is therefore incorrect. The defence of duress will only apply where the defendant was forced to commit an offence to avoid death or serious injury (*R* v *Conway* [1989] RTR 35). The defence *will not* apply in cases of criminal damage or where criminal damage has been threatened, no matter how serious. Answers A and C are therefore incorrect.

Road Policing, para. 3.2.13

Answer 2.25

Answer **C** — A person may claim the defence of 'necessity' when charged with a drink driving offence. The situation was considered in the cases of *DPP* v *Tomkinson* [2001] RTR 38 and *DPP* v *Hicks* [2002] EWHC 1638. In *Hicks*, the court found that the defence would be available only if:

- the driving was undertaken to avoid consequences that could not otherwise have been avoided;
- those consequences were inevitable and involved a risk of serious harm to the driver *or someone else for whom he or she was responsible*;
- the driver did no more than reasonably necessary to avoid harm; *and*
- the danger of so driving was not disproportionate to the harm threatened.

This ruling followed the earlier *Tomkinson* case, when the Divisional Court found that the defendant had driven a far greater distance than was necessary to avoid the relevant danger and that the defence would not be available. In the case examined in the question, unquestionably the daughter had been threatened with serious harm. The harm threatened must be serious, not just immediate and unlawful, therefore answer A is incorrect. The defence *may* be used where a person other than the driver is threatened, therefore answer B is incorrect. However, it could be argued that the distance JOHN travelled after picking up his daughter was greater than necessary and that he could have stopped at some point to call the police, which is why answer C is correct and answer D is incorrect.

Road Policing, para. 3.2.13

3 Notices of Intended Prosecution

Please note that the questions in this chapter relate to material in the Blackstone's Police Manuuals which has been excluded from the Inspectors' Exam syllabus for 2008.

STUDY PREPARATION

Like much road traffic legislation, the law governing notices of intended prosecution (NIPs) is concerned with procedural detail. Once you know which offences are generally covered by the NIP procedure, you then need to learn the procedure required for proper service to be accepted by the courts and any exceptions provided for.

Understanding the purpose behind NIPs will help you in learning all this important procedural detail.

QUESTIONS

Question 3.1

Constable DALTON was following a car being driven by a person whom he recognised as being GIBSON. GIBSON failed to stop for the officer and, following a pursuit, Constable DALTON lost sight of the car. The officer knew GIBSON's home address and attended there straight away, in order to report him for driving without due care and attention. There was no reply at the house. Constable DALTON eventually caught up with GIBSON two days later.

What action should the officer now take, to comply with s. 1 of the Road Traffic Offenders Act 1988 (notice of intended prosecution (NIP))?

A Issue a verbal NIP personally to GIBSON there and then.

B Send a written NIP or summons to GIBSON within 12 days.

C Send both a written NIP and summons to GIBSON within 14 days.

D Send a written NIP or summons to GIBSON within 14 days.

Question 3.2

ALLAN has been given a verbal warning, at the time she committed an offence, of a notice of intended prosecution (NIP).

What proof is required that she understood the notice?

A It is for the prosecution to prove that the defendant understood the notice on every occasion.

B If the defendant claims he or she did not understand a verbal notice, it is for the defence to prove this fact.

C It is for the prosecution to prove that the defendant understood the notice, if a written notice was not given at a later date.

D It is for the prosecution to prove that the defendant understood the notice, if the defendant disputes this fact.

Question 3.3

A vehicle was caught activating a speed detection camera in the Eastshire area. A notice under s. 172 of the Road Traffic Act 1988 was sent to the registered keeper, YOUNG, who lived in the Westshire area, requesting the driver details. YOUNG was, in fact, the driver of the vehicle at the time of the offence, but decided to ignore the request and failed to reply to the notice.

Considering the original offence (exceeding the speed limit) took place in Eastshire, could both cases be heard in Westshire where the second offence (failing to reply to the notice) took place?

A No, as the two offences were not part of an ongoing incident.

B Yes, but only if the court considers the second offence to be more serious.

C Yes, the cases may be heard in either court.

D No, the cases must be heard in a court where the original offence took place.

Question 3.4

Constable SULSTON attended an accident which had been reported in the High Street, where HAMMOND, who was riding a pedal cycle, had knocked over and injured an elderly person on a Pelican Crossing. Constable SULSTON decided to report HAMMOND for the offence of causing bodily harm by wanton or furious driving a vehicle, under s. 35 of the Offences Against the Person Act 1861.

Should Constable SULSTON give HAMMOND a verbal notice of intended prosecution (NIP), in these circumstances?

A No, but a NIP would have been required if HAMMOND had been reported for dangerous, careless or inconsiderate cycling.

B No, NIPs are not required in relation to offences committed with pedal cycles.

C Yes, a NIP is required as the accident involved a pedal cycle and not a motor vehicle.

D Yes, a NIP is required for dangerous, careless or inconsiderate cycling, or any other similar offence.

Question 3.5

PRIDEAUX was dealt with by Constable ROACH for an offence of leaving a vehicle in a dangerous position. Constable ROACH issued PRIDEAUX with a fixed penalty notice for the offence; however, the constable did not serve PRIDEAUX with a verbal notice of intended prosecution (NIP) at the time of issuing the notice.

Has Constable ROACH acted correctly in these circumstances?

A No, but a written NIP may still be served on PRIDEAUX for the prosecution to proceed.

B No, a verbal NIP should have been served when the fixed penalty notice was issued.

C Yes, there was no requirement to serve a verbal or written NIP in these circumstances.

D Yes, this is not an offence which requires a NIP to be served, whether verbal or written.

Question 3.6

HAWKLEY was responsible for failing to stop after an accident in a supermarket car park, when he damaged another car and drove off. A witness took his registration number and reported the accident to Constable DAVIES. The officer sent a notice of intended prosecution (NIP), to HAWKLEY's address as shown on Police National Computer (PNC). However, HAWKLEY had moved. HAWKLEY was traced two months later and, when interviewed, stated he had never received the NIP.

What effect would the failure to serve the NIP have on any future prosecution against HAWKLEY?

A None, as HAWKLEY was at fault for the failure of the service.

B The NIP was not served in time and therefore the case cannot proceed.

C None, a NIP was not required as the offence occurred at the time of an accident.

D None, a NIP was not required as the accident did not occur on a road.

Question 3.7

LEWINSKI was driving his motor vehicle along a main road, approaching a set of traffic lights at a junction. Due to a lack of concentration, LEWINSKI drove through a red light and collided with a heavy goods vehicle. LEWINSKI suffered severe head injuries as a result of the accident and was taken to hospital, where he remained for several weeks. Because of his injuries, LEWINSKI was not able to recall being involved in the accident. The officer in the case is contemplating whether or not a notice of intended prosecution (NIP) should be served on LEWINSKI, for driving through the red light.

Would the officer be correct in serving an NIP because of the serious injuries, in these circumstances?

A Yes, as LEWINSKI was severely injured as a result of the accident.

B No, a NIP is never required when the driver has been involved in an accident.

C It is immaterial whether he was injured or not, because the accident was not of a minor nature.

D Yes, a NIP is always required when the driver is injured as a result of an accident.

Question 3.8

GODDARD has been summonsed to court for an offence of careless driving.

What evidential proof will be required by the court, that GODDARD has been served with a notice of intended prosecution (NIP), under s. 1(1) of the Road Traffic Offenders Act 1988?

A The prosecution must show that the requirements of s. 1(1) of the 1988 Act have been complied with through oral testimony.

B The prosecution must show that the requirements of s. 1(1) of the 1988 Act have been complied with through documentary evidence.

C The court will always assume that the requirements of s. 1(1) of the 1988 Act have been complied with.

D The court will always assume that the requirements of s. 1(1) of the 1988 Act have been complied with until the contrary is proved.

Question 3.9

Notices of intended prosecution (NIP) are served under s. 1 of the Road Traffic Offenders Act 1988.

In which of the following scenarios will an NIP have not been served correctly?

A A NIP was served personally by the officer in the case on the defendant's common law husband.

B The officer in the case was aware that the defendant was of no fixed abode and applied to the court immediately for a summons to be issued, without making efforts to serve the notice personally.

C The defendant was in hospital for six weeks. The officer in the case was aware of this but still served a written NIP to the defendant's home address, while the defendant was away.

D An officer gave a verbal NIP to a motorist, who later claimed that the officer had not specified what offence he was being prosecuted for and was only told that he had committed a 'speeding offence'.

ANSWERS

Answer 3.1

Answer **B** — Under s. 1 of the Road Traffic Offenders Act 1988, before certain offences can be prosecuted, the defendant must have *either* been warned of the possibility of prosecution at the time of the offence, *or* served with a summons (or charged) within 14 days of the offence *or* a notice of intended prosecution (NIP) must have been sent to the registered keeper within 14 days of the offence.

Answer A is incorrect as a verbal NIP may only be given at the time of the offence. If this is not possible, the prosecution is able to send a written one to the keeper's last known address.

Answer C is incorrect as there is no requirement to send both the summons and the written NIP within 14 days; one will suffice. Answer C is also incorrect, as is answer D, because two days have already elapsed since the incident, and the written NIP (or summons) must be sent within 14 days of the offence committed.

Road Policing, para. 3.3.1

Answer 3.2

Answer **A** — If a verbal warning is given at the time of the offence, it must be shown that the defendant understood it (*Gibson* v *Dalton* [1980] RTR 410). Proof that the defendant understood the warning will lie with the prosecution. Answer B is incorrect. The prosecution must show this on *every* occasion, whether or not the defendant claims he or she did not understand, or whether a written notice was given at a later date. Answers C and D are therefore incorrect.

Road Policing, para. 3.3.1

Answer 3.3

Answer **C** — When an offence is committed partly within the jurisdiction of two different courts, it may be heard in *either* court (*Kennet DC* v *Young* [1999] RTR 235). Answers A, B and D are therefore incorrect.

Road Policing, para. 3.3.1

Answer 3.4

Answer **A** — There is a list of offences which require a NIP contained in sch. 1 to the Road Traffic Offenders Act 1988 and these include dangerous, careless or inconsiderate cycling. Answer B is therefore incorrect.

However, the list of offences in sch. 1 is exhaustive and other offences, even if similar in nature to those in the list, will *not* be covered by the requirements of s. 1(1) (*Sulston* v *Hammond* [1970] 1 WLR 1164). Answer D is incorrect.

Section 2(1) of the Road Traffic Offenders Act 1988 states that the requirement to serve an NIP does not apply in relation to an offence if, at the time, or immediately afterwards and owing to the presence of the *vehicle* concerned on a road an accident occurred. Therefore, had HAMMOND been reported for dangerous, careless or inconsiderate cycling (and not the offence under s. 35 above), an NIP would *not* have been required. Answer C is therefore incorrect.

Road Policing, paras 3.3.2, 3.2.3

Answer 3.5

Answer **C** — The offences which require a NIP are listed in sch. 1 to the Road Traffic Offenders Act 1988. The list includes leaving a vehicle in a dangerous position; therefore, answer D is incorrect.

Section 2 of the Road Traffic Offenders Act 1988 contains a list of exemptions from the requirement to serve a NIP (whether written or verbal). Under s. 2(2)(a), there is no requirement to serve a NIP in relation to an offence in respect of which a fixed penalty notice has been given, or fixed. Answers A and B are therefore incorrect.

Road Policing, paras 3.3.2, 3.3.3

Answer 3.6

Answer **A** — Section 2(1) of the Road Traffic Offenders Act 1988 states that a notice of intended prosecution (NIP) does not need to be served if at the time or immediately afterwards and owing to the presence of the motor vehicle concerned *on a road* a accident occurred. This means that where an accident occurs on a road, a NIP is not required for a due care offence; however, where an accident occurs in a public place a NIP *will be* required. Answers C and D are therefore incorrect.

A notice must be served on the defendant within 14 days of the offence, if it was not given verbally at the time. However, under s. 2(3) of the 1988 Act, if the defendant contributes to the failure to serve the NIP, then that will not be a bar to his or her conviction. Answer B is therefore incorrect.

Road Policing, para. 3.3.3

Answer 3.7

Answer **C** — Generally, a notice of intended prosecution (NIP) is *not* required if at the time of the offence, or immediately afterwards, an accident occurred owing to the presence of a motor vehicle on a road (s. 2(1) of the Road Traffic Offenders Act 1988). However, there is an exception to this rule. Where the driver of a motor vehicle is unaware that an accident has taken place because it is so minor, there *will* be a need to serve a NIP (*Bentley* v *Dickinson* [1983] RTR 356). Answer B is incorrect, as the exception shows that sometimes a NIP may be required following an accident.

When the accident is so severe that the driver of the vehicle is unable to recall it, a NIP is *not* required (*DPP* v *Pidhajeckyi* [1991] RTR 136). Answer A is incorrect because of the ruling in this case. Answer D is incorrect, as there is nothing in the Act stating that a NIP is required every time a driver is injured in an accident.

Answer C is *correct* because it is *not* relevant whether the driver was injured, as the accident was not of a minor nature (and *Bentley* does not apply), and therefore it falls within the scope of s. 2(1) (above).

Road Policing, para. 3.3.3

Answer 3.8

Answer **D** — Section 1 of the Road Traffic Offenders Act 1988 relates to the notice or warning in relation to notices of intended prosecution (NIP).

Subsection (3) of this section relates to a presumption in relation to NIPs, in that:

> (3) The requirement of subsection (1) above shall in every case be deemed to have been complied with unless and until the contrary is proved.

The effect of s. 1(3), therefore, is to place the burden of proving failure to comply with the section on the defence on a balance of probabilities. Answer C is therefore incorrect. The prosecution have no such evidential burden. Answers A and B are therefore incorrect.

Road Policing, para. 3.3.4

Answer 3.9

Answer **B** — Answers A, C and D are all based on decided cases, where the court agreed that the provisions of s. 1 had been complied with. If you selected any of these answers, you would have been incorrect.

Section 1 of the Road Traffic Offenders Act 1988 states:

(1A) A notice required by this section to be served on any person may be served on that person —
- (a) by delivering it to him;
- (b) by addressing it to him and leaving it at his last known address; or
- (c) by sending it by registered post, recorded delivery service or first class post addressed to him at his last known address.

(2) A notice shall be deemed for the purposes of subsection (1)(c) above to have been served on a person if it was sent by registered post or recorded delivery service addressed to him at his last known address, notwithstanding that the notice was returned as undelivered or was for any other reason not received by him.

(3) The requirement of subsection (1) above shall in every case be deemed to have been complied with unless and until the contrary is proved.

Answer A is based on the case of *Hosier* v *Goodall* [1962] 1 All ER 30. A notice served on the defendant's spouse or partner was sufficient. Answer C originates from *Phipps* v *McCormick* [1972] Crim LR 540. If the defendant is not at his or her home address, for instance because he or she is in hospital or on holiday, service to his or her last known address will suffice, even if the police are aware of that fact. Answer D comes from the case of *Pope* v *Clarke* [1953] 2 All ER 704. The purpose of the notice is to alert the defendant to the likelihood of prosecution. It is not necessary to specify which offence is being considered; it is enough that the defendant is made aware of the *nature* of the offence.

If neither the defendant nor the registered keeper have any fixed abode, reasonable efforts must be made to serve the notice personally. If such efforts fail, s. 2(3) would apply and the need for service would be removed. Since the officer in the answer did not make reasonable efforts to trace the defendant, the NIP was not served.

Road Policing, para. 3.3.5

4 Accidents and Collisions

STUDY PREPARATION

The law relating to road traffic 'accidents' is primarily concerned with obligations on the drivers involved and the offences for failing to comply with those obligations. Throughout this chapter we will use the term 'road traffic collision', which is in line with current policing practice.

The most important bit of this subject is knowing what amounts to an 'accident' or 'collision'. You need to be able to recognise from the fact pattern of a question whether an 'accident' has happened. Then you need to know what obligations the law imposes and upon whom. You also need to know any offences which may apply, along with the attendant police powers.

QUESTIONS

Question 4.1

SULLIVAN and his friend HARRIS drove to the local shops. SULLIVAN was driving, although both had consumed 4 pints of cider. They parked outside a shop at the top of a hill and SULLIVAN went inside, leaving HARRIS in the passenger seat, saying 'I'll be back now'. For a joke HARRIS let off the handbrake and let the car roll down hill. HARRIS did not touch the steering wheel but unfortunately the car was travelling so fast that when he tried to apply the handbrake to stop it, it failed and the car collided with a pedestrian, severely injuring them. SULLIVAN saw this from the top of the hill and ran off, fearing being breathalysed, straight past the local police station.

What is SULLIVAN's responsibility, under s. 170 of the Road Traffic Act 1988, in these circumstances?

A SULLIVAN has no responsibility under s. 170, as he was not the driver at the time of the accident.

B SULLIVAN has no responsibility under s. 170, as by operating the handbrake HARRIS assumed the driver's responsibility.

C SULLIVAN committed offences of failing to stop and failing to report contrary to s. 170.

D SULLIVAN committed offences of failing to stop and failing to report contrary to s. 170, in addition to perverting the course of justice.

Question 4.2

While driving his car, DAWSON was involved in a road traffic collision with a motor cycle being ridden by WINTER. WINTER suffered cuts and grazes as a result. The drivers exchanged details and WINTER asked DAWSON for his insurance certificate. DAWSON did not have it with him, but gave WINTER the name of his insurance company and promised to show him the certificate the next day.

Has DAWSON complied with the requirements of s. 170 of the Road Traffic Act 1988 in these circumstances?

A Yes, he is not obliged to produce his insurance certificate to another driver, provided he gives the name of his insurance company.

B No, he must report the collision to the police as soon as reasonably practicable, and produce his insurance certificate within seven days.

C No, he must report the collision to the police as soon as reasonably practicable, and produce his insurance certificate at the same time.

D Yes, provided he produces his insurance certificate to WINTER within 24 hours.

Question 4.3

BENNETT was involved in a road traffic collision, while driving his employer's van. He drove into the rear of a car at a set of traffic lights. BENNETT was asked by the driver of the other vehicle for his name and address only. BENNETT gave his own name, but gave his employer's address as he was driving a works vehicle.

Has BENNETT complied with s. 170(2) of the Road Traffic Act 1988 (duty to stop and give details) in these circumstances?

A No, he should also have given the name of the owner of the vehicle to the other driver.

B No, he should also have given the name of the owner of the vehicle, and the registration number to the other driver.

C Yes, he has complied fully with the requirements of the Act in these circumstances.

D No, he should have given his own address to the other driver, not his employer's.

Question 4.4

McQUIRTER was involved in a road traffic collision (RTC) where he aquaplaned on a wet road and hit a brick wall. He suffered whiplash injuries from the force of the spin and slight shock; his passenger, however, was uninjured. There were no other vehicles involved and the wall was undamaged. However, a bystander witnessed the incident. McQUIRTER drove straight home where he saw his neighbour, an off-duty police officer, in the garden and told her about the incident. Shortly afterwards an on-duty police officer attended McQUIRTER's address as a result of a call from the witness. McQUIRTER told the officer he was just about to go to the police station and told the officer about the incident.

At what point, if any, did McQUIRTER comply with the requirements of s. 170 of the Road Traffic Act 1988 (reporting accidents)?

A At no point, but he did not have to comply with s. 170.

B At no point, and he committed two separate offences in relation to s. 170.

C When he told a police officer; the fact she was off-duty is immaterial.

D When he told the on-duty police officer who arrived at his house.

Question 4.5

CAWTHORN was driving his car and towing a trailer, when he stopped at a shop on the brow of a hill. While he was inside the shop, the coupling which fixed the trailer to the car broke. The trailer rolled down the hill and collided with a parked car causing damage to it.

What obligation does CAWTHORN have to exchange details with the driver of the parked vehicle in these circumstances?

A None, as he was not to blame for the accident.

B He has an obligation to stop and exchange details with the owner.

C None, as he was not driving a vehicle at the time of the accident.

D None, as the trailer is not a mechanically propelled vehicle.

Question 4.6

CUTTER was involved in a collision in a multi-storey car park, which was open to the public at the time. CUTTER was driving out of a parking space in his van when he scraped the side of a parked car. CUTTER failed to stop after the accident; however, a witness noted his registration number. When he was traced by the police, CUTTER stated that he had not stopped as he was unaware of the collision.

Who would have responsibility for proving or disproving that CUTTER was unaware of the collision?

A The defence must show that on the balance of probabilities he was unaware of the collision.

B The prosecution must show beyond reasonable doubt that he would have been aware of the collision.

C The defence must show beyond reasonable doubt that he was unaware of the collision.

D The question is not relevant; there was no requirement to stop after the collision as it did not occur on a road.

Question 4.7

HANKS was driving a car along a quiet country road. HANKS collided with a parked car while negotiating a bend, causing damage to it. HANKS waited at the scene of the collision for 30 minutes, but no other people passed by.

How must HANKS now report the collision to the police?

A At a police station or to a constable within 24 hours of it occurring.

B At a police station or to a constable as soon as practicable.

C To the police within 24 hours of failing to find the owner of the other vehicle.

D At a police station as soon as practicable.

Question 4.8

POWELL was involved in a road traffic collision, having driven into the rear of a parked and unattended vehicle.

What duties are imposed on POWELL, under s. 170(2) of the Road Traffic Act 1988, in respect of providing details to the owner of the other vehicle?

A POWELL must remain at the scene for such a time as would allow the owner or keeper of the other vehicle to ask for the information.

B POWELL must remain at the scene for such a time as would allow the owner of the other vehicle to ask for the information.

C POWELL must remain at the scene for such a time as would allow any person to ask for the information.

D POWELL must remain at the scene for such a time as would allow anyone having reasonable grounds for so requiring, to ask for the information.

Question 4.9

KEOWN was involved in a road traffic collision at 2.00 am when she drove into a tree, causing damage to it. There was nobody about at this time and KEOWN, who had been drinking, drove off without stopping, to a friend's house, where she telephoned the police station. KEOWN spoke to Constable FARRAR and reported the details of the accident and gave her own details, but refused to say where she was. She said that she would attend the police station in the morning to give further details. KEOWN arrived at the police station at 10.00 am and reported the accident to MUNROE, a station enquiry clerk.

Has KEOWN complied with the requirements of s. 170 of the Road Traffic Act 1988 (duty to report an accident) in these circumstances?

A No, the accident was not reported as soon as practicable.
B No, the accident was not reported to a police officer.
C Yes, the accident was reported within 24 hours of the telephone call.
D No, the accident was not reported to a police officer in uniform.

Question 4.10

HULL is employed as a care worker for the elderly. HULL drove BROOKFIELD (aged 85 years) to a shopping centre but had to brake sharply to avoid a collision with a dog that ran out in front of the car. The dog was not injured but BROOKFIELD (seated in the front passenger seat) suffered shock and HULL suffered whiplash as a consequence of the incident. HULL and BROOKFIELD were taken to the hospital by a passing motorist, but both were released after a few hours. HULL did not contact the police. Two days later, BROOKFIELD's daughter found out about the incident and contacted the police.

Would HULL be guilty of an offence under s. 170(4) of the Road Traffic Act 1988, (failing to report an accident) in these circumstances?

A No, because the personal injuries were caused to people in HULL's car only.
B Yes, the offence is complete.
C No, the shock suffered by BROOKFIELD is not classed as a personal injury.
D No, because HULL had to attend the hospital for treatment also.

Question 4.11

KNIGHT was involved in a road traffic collision where another vehicle ran into the back of her on the motorway. Several other vehicles narrowly avoided the collision, as the motorway was very busy. KNIGHT had no physical injury but was clearly shaken up by the incident. She did not visit the hospital, or her doctor. Three weeks later she still has no physical injury, however, she is still having flashbacks and is having trouble sleeping and is displaying other psychological signs of distress.

Was KNIGHT 'injured' as per s. 170 of the Road Traffic Act 1988 in relation to her current medical condition?

A No, as this only applies to physical injury.

B No, as her condition was not obvious at the time of the accident.

C Yes, psychological harm may well amount to such injury.

D Yes, but *only* because KNIGHT was in shock at the scene.

Question 4.12

Constable ANGEL was investigating a road traffic collision (RTC), during which a pedestrian was injured while crossing the road. The driver of the offending vehicle, ROPER, failed to stop at the scene; however, a witness noted the registration number of his vehicle and formed the opinion that the driver had been drinking due to the way he drove the vehicle away. Constable ANGEL immediately attended ROPER's home address and the vehicle was parked outside. The officer spoke to ROPER's neighbour who stated that she saw ROPER stagger as if drunk from his car and enter his house.

What powers are available to Constable ANGEL, to deal with ROPER in these circumstances?

A The officer can proceed only by way of summons, as failing to stop at an injury RTC is not an indictable offence.

B There is a power of arrest, however there is no power of entry as failing to stop at an injury RTC is not an indictable offence.

C There is a power of entry, but only to breathalyse the driver.

D There is a power of entry and a power of arrest.

Question 4.13

A male is suspected of an offence of dangerous cycling by riding quickly on a busy footway, and Sergeant AZIZ is investigating. Sergeant AZIZ asks the male for his name and address for the purposes of summonsing him for the offence. When asked the male says nothing and just stands and looks at the officer. The officer is aware that there is an offence of refusing to give, or giving false details after allegation of dangerous or careless driving or cycling contrary to s. 168 of the Road Traffic Act 1988.

In the circumstances as outlined has this offence been committed?

A Yes, as failure to give details amounts to refusal.

B Yes, silence has been held to be a refusal in these circumstances.

C No, the offence is only committed by those who refuse to, or give false details.

D No, as this offence only relates to where the dangerous cycling involves a collision.

ANSWERS

Answer 4.1

Answer **C** — The Divisional Court has held that the offence under s. 170(4) (failing to stop or report an accident) is not a 'driving offence' as such and does not require that the person be 'driving' at the time. Arguments as to whether HARRIS ever 'drives' the vehicle are extraneous therefore.

Even though there may be a break in the actual driving of the vehicle, the driver may still be under the obligations imposed by s. 170 if an accident occurs while he/she is away from the vehicle. Therefore, where a driver left his vehicle on a road with its hazard warning lights on while he ran to a post box and the vehicle coasted downhill into a wall, the driver still had a duty to report the accident under s. 170 (*Cawthorn* v *DPP* [2000] RTR 45). In *Cawthorn*, even the fact that a passenger may have been directly responsible for the accident (by letting off the handbrake), it was held that the circumstances met the requirements of s. 170 and that the driver attracted the relevant statutory duties; answers A and B are therefore incorrect. Had SULLIVAN run straight into the police station he may have complied with his duty to report, but no doubt scored an 'own goal' with the breathalyser procedure!

The Court of Appeal has refused to accept that a driver who failed to stop and report an accident for fear of being breathalysed did not, without more, commit an offence of perverting the course of justice (*R* v *Clark* [2003] EWCA 991); therefore answer D is incorrect.

Road Policing, paras 3.4.2, 3.4.3

Answer 4.2

Answer **C** — If a driver is involved in a collision where injury is caused to another person, he or she must, at the time of the collision, produce a certificate of insurance to a constable *or* any person having reasonable grounds for requiring it (s. 170(5) of the Road Traffic Act 1988). Answer A is therefore incorrect.

If the driver does not produce his or her insurance certificate as required above, he or she *must* report the accident to the police *and* produce an insurance certificate as soon as practicable, and in any case within 24 hours (s. 170(6)).

Answer D is incorrect as once a driver fails to produce a certificate at the scene to the other driver, the requirement moves to reporting the collision and producing the certificate to the police.

Answer B is incorrect as the requirement is to report the collision *and* produce the insurance certificate as soon as practicable and within 24 hours. Under s. 170(7) of the 1988 Act, a person will escape prosecution for failing to produce insurance at the time of the collision, or later at the police station, if he or she produces it within seven days from the collision (usually as a result of the issue of an HO/RT/1). Therefore, although answer B may appear correct, the *first* process must be to report the collision and produce the certificate as soon as practicable.

Road Policing, para. 3.4.2

Answer 4.3

Answer **C** — Under s. 170(2) of the Road Traffic Act 1988, the driver of a vehicle involved in a road traffic collision must stop and *if required to do so* by some person having reasonable grounds, give his or her name and address and also the name and address of the owner of the vehicle, and the registration mark of the vehicle.

Because the driver of the other vehicle did not ask for the name of the owner and the registration mark, BENNETT commits no offence by failing to give them. Answers A and B are therefore incorrect.

It has been held that, as the reason for the requirement to 'exchange details' is to allow future communications between parties, the address of the driver's solicitor would satisfy the requirements of s. 170(2) (*DPP* v *McCarthy* [1999] RTR 323). Answer D is therefore incorrect.

Road Policing, para. 3.4.2

Answer 4.4

Answer **A** — Section 170 of the Road Traffic Act 1988 states:

(1) This section applies in a case where, owing to the presence of a mechanically propelled vehicle on a road or other public place, an accident occurs by which —
  - (a) personal injury is caused to a person other than the driver of that mechanically propelled vehicle, or
  - (b) damage is caused —
    - (i) to a vehicle other than that mechanically propelled vehicle or a trailer drawn by that mechanically propelled vehicle, or
    - (ii) to an animal other than an animal in or on that mechanically propelled vehicle or a trailer drawn by that mechanically propelled vehicle, or

(iii) to any other property constructed on, fixed to, growing in or otherwise forming part of the land on which the road or place in question is situated or land adjacent to such land...

Applying this principle only the driver is injured; damage is not caused to another vehicle, roadside property or animal. In the circumstances of the scenario s. 170 does not apply to McQUIRTER and he has done nothing wrong; therefore answers B, C and D are incorrect.

Note however that had subs. (1) applied in these circumstances, McQUIRTER's duty to stop and report is probably not discharged by waiting until the police call at his house and then telling them (see *Dawson* v *Winter* (1932) 49 TLR 128 *obiter*); neither is it discharged if the driver tells a friend who happens to be a police officer (*Mutton* v *Bates (No. 1)* [1984] RTR 256).

Road Policing, para. 3.4.2

Answer 4.5

Answer **B** — It has been held that even though a driver may not have been to blame for a collision, he or she will still attract the duties imposed by s. 170 of the Road Traffic Act 1988 (*Harding* v *Price* [1948] 1 All ER 283). Answer A is therefore incorrect.

If there has been a break from driving, and a collision occurs while the driver is away from the vehicle, he or she will still be required to fulfil the obligations of s. 170 (*Cawthorn* v *DPP* [2000] RTR 45). In this case, even though the driver was not directly responsible for the accident (the passenger had let off the handbrake), there was still a requirement to comply with s. 170. Answer C is incorrect as there is no requirement for a person to be driving at the time of the accident.

Answer D is incorrect as s. 170(1) requires the driver to stop and exchange details when damage was caused to another vehicle by his or her own vehicle, or a trailer being drawn by it.

Road Policing, para. 3.4.2

Answer 4.6

Answer **A** — The case of *Cutter* v *Eagle Star Insurance Co. Ltd* [1998] 4 All ER 417 changed the requirements under s. 170 of the Road Traffic Act 1988. Prior to this case, a collision was not 'reportable' unless it occurred on a road. The section has now been extended to include 'public places'. Since the car park was open to any member of the public, it was a public place and covered by s. 170. Answer D is therefore incorrect.

When a driver alleges he or she was unaware that a collision had taken place, it is for the defence to show *on the balance of probabilities* that this was the case (*Selby* v *Chief Constable of Avon and Somerset* [1988] RTR 216). Answers B and C are therefore incorrect.

Road Policing, para. 3.4.2

Answer 4.7

Answer **B** — Under s. 170(2) of the Road Traffic Act 1988, the driver of the mechanically propelled vehicle must stop and, if required to do so by any person having reasonable grounds for so requiring, give his or her name and address and also the name and address of the owner and the identification marks of the vehicle. If for any reason the driver of the mechanically propelled vehicle does not give his or her name and address under subsection (2) above, he/she must report the accident (s. 170(3)).

Under s. 170(6), to comply with the above duty, the driver —

(a) must do so at a police station or to a constable, and

(b) must do so as soon as is reasonably practicable and, in any case, within twenty-four hours of the occurrence of the accident.

The requirement is to report the collision at a police station *or* to a constable (answer D is incorrect). This must be done as soon as reasonably practicable (and it will be for the court to decide what is reasonable), and in any case within 24 hours of the occurrence of the accident, therefore, answer C is incorrect.

This does not give the driver 24 hours to report the collision — and in most circumstances there is no reason for a collision not to be reported straight away because of the availability of police officers 24 hours a day. Answer A is therefore incorrect.

Road Policing, para. 3.4.2

Answer 4.8

Answer **D** — Under s. 170(2) of the Road Traffic Act 1988, the driver of the mechanically propelled vehicle must stop and, if required to do so by any person having reasonable grounds for so requiring, give his or her name and address and also the name and address of the owner and the identification marks of the vehicle. This might be the owner, the keeper or anybody else who has reasonable grounds (answers A and B are incorrect). However, s. 170(2) above does not state that the driver must wait around for any person; therefore, answer C is incorrect.

Road Policing, para. 3.4.2

Answer 4.9

Answer **A** — Under s. 170(3) of the Road Traffic Act 1988, if the driver of a motor vehicle involved in an accident on a road does not give his or her name and address at the scene, he or she must report the accident. The accident must be reported as soon as is reasonably practicable and, in any case, within 24 hours of the occurrence of the accident.

The accident must be reported in person (and not by telephone — see *Wisdom* v *MacDonald* [1983] RTR 186). Answer C is incorrect. The accident must be reported either to a police officer, or at a police station. Since the choice is given, reporting the matter to a station enquiry clerk would seem to comply with s. 170. It is not, however, necessary for the police officer to be in uniform. Answers B and D are therefore incorrect.

Road Policing, paras 3.4.2, 3.4.2.3

Answer 4.10

Answer **B** — If the driver of the vehicle is the only person injured then the accident will not be reportable; it will, however, be reportable if the passenger in the vehicle is injured. The fact that BROOKFIELD suffered shock would be an injury for the purposes of s. 170(4) of the Road Traffic Act 1988 and, therefore, HULL was under a duty to stop and report the accident, making answers A and C incorrect.

It was held in *DPP* v *Hay* [2006] RTR 3 that the requirement under s. 170(4) is not negated either by police attendance at the scene of the accident, or by the driver being taken to hospital. Answer D is therefore incorrect.

Road Policing, paras 3.4.2, 3.4.2.2, 3.4.3

Answer 4.11

Answer **C** — Injury under s. 170 will obviously apply to physical injury, in addition it has been held to include shock; answer A is therefore incorrect. Given comparable developments in the area of assaults (e.g. *R* v *Ireland* [1997] 3 WLR 534; *R* v *Chan-Fook* [1994] 1 WLR 689), it would appear that psychological harm may well amount to an 'injury' for these purposes. Such injuries are not necessarily obvious at the time, but this does not mean that they are not classed as such; answer B is therefore incorrect.

Although shock has been deemed to be 'injury', it is not a precondition to further psychological harm and therefore answer D is incorrect.

Road Policing, para. 3.4.2.2

Answer 4.12

Answer **D** — A driver who fails to stop after a road traffic collision commits an offence under s. 170 of the Road Traffic Act 1988. Under s. 71 of the Criminal Justice and Police Act 2001, the offence of failing to stop following a personal injury road traffic collision became an arrestable offence; however the Serious Organised Crime and Police Act 2005 changed powers of arrest and now no offence is arrestable, although arrests can be made for all offences provided the officer could show it was 'necessary'. In addition the power of entry under s. 17 of the Police and Criminal Evidence Act 1984 was also amended by the Serious Organised Crime and Police Act 2005 to reflect this change in the term 'arrestable offence', replacing that term with 'indictable offence'. Section 170 is not one of the statutes now mentioned in s. 17, and although you could arrest for this offence, there is no longer a specific power of arrest as s. 170 is not an indictable offence.

However the Serious Organised Crime and Police Act 2005 has not affected s. 6E of the Road Traffic Act 1988, which allows that:

> A constable may enter any place (using reasonable force if necessary) for the purpose of—
>
> (a) imposing a requirement by virtue of section 6(5) following an accident in a case where the constable reasonably suspects that the accident involved injury of any person, or
>
> (b) arresting a person under section 6D following an accident in a case where the constable reasonably suspects that the accident involved injury of any person.

In order for this power to apply it must be shown that:

- there was an accident (mere suspicion or belief by the officer, however strong, is not enough);
- the officer reasonably believed that the person had been driving, attempting to drive or in charge of the vehicle concerned (suspicion is not enough);

- the officer reasonably suspected that the accident involved injury to any person — including the driver (for this part suspicion is enough provided it is reasonable).

These facts are outlined in the scenario and there is power of entry and arrest; answers A, B and C are therefore incorrect.

Road Policing, para. 3.4.3

Answer 4.13

Answer **C** — The requirement to provide details arises where the driver (or rider) is alleged to have committed an offence of dangerous or careless driving or cycling, as is the case here.

There is, however, no requirement for an accident/collision of any sort to have occurred for the legislation to take effect; answer D is therefore incorrect.

The section uses the word 'refuses' but makes no mention of a failure to provide the required details. Section 11 of the Road Traffic Act 1988 states:

(1) The following provisions apply for the interpretation of sections 3A to 10 of this Act.

(2) In those sections —
'drug' includes any intoxicant other than alcohol,
'fail' includes refuse...

The interpretation of 'fail' in s. 11 of the Road Traffic Act 1988 only applies to ss. 3A to 10 of the Act, and not to s. 168 and although subs. (2) makes provision for a 'failure' to include a 'refusal' (in relation to drink driving offences), the Act says nothing about a vice versa situation. Given that omission, together with the fact that the courts have held (albeit in an employment law case) that 'failure' is not synonymous with 'refusal' (see *Lowson* v *Percy Main & District Social Club and Institute Ltd* [1979] ICR 568), it would seem that a mere failure to provide the details required under s. 168 will not amount to the offence above. Answers A and B are therefore incorrect.

You should not get confused with the fact that there is no separate offence committed under the 1988 Act, the original offence is still committed and there is existing legislation to take the offender to court to answer that charge.

Road Policing, para. 3.4.3

5 Drink, Drugs and Driving

STUDY PREPARATION

This is a big one. The areas of law and procedure covered in this chapter are extensive. You will need to know the elements of each of the main drink driving offences first. Entwined with those offences is a range of police powers such as the powers to require breath samples. Recent changes to the Road Traffic Act 1988 allow police officers to administer three preliminary tests — a breath test, a test indicating whether a person is unfit to drive due to drink or drugs, and a test to detect the presence of drugs in a person's body. Failure or refusal to comply with such requirements can lead to further offences and further powers. It is sometimes helpful to divide this subject area into roadside, police station and hospital procedures.

The evidential issues are also important and there is a great deal of established case law to clarify this area of the legislation.

QUESTIONS

Question 5.1

GUILLAM has been convicted in the magistrates' court for an offence of driving with excess alcohol, having been found to be twice the prescribed limit. GUILLAM was convicted of the same offence six years previously, and was banned from driving.

Do the circumstances above mean that GUILLAM may be required to take part in the High Risk Offender Scheme?

A Possibly, but it would depend on the level of alcohol that was in GUILLAM's body in the previous case.

B Yes, because it is GUILLAM's second conviction in 10 years.

C No, because it is not GUILLAM's second conviction in 5 years.

D No, because it is not GUILLAM's third conviction in 10 years.

Question 5.2

The police were called to a country lane, where they found an unattended vehicle, which had driven through a hedge into a farmer's field. Constable WINTER found HUNTLEY walking approximately a mile from the vehicle. HUNTLEY admitted being the owner of the vehicle, but stated he had not been driving it that night; he would not say who had been. Suspecting that he had been driving the vehicle, Constable WINTER breathalysed HUNTLEY, and the result was positive.

Would Constable WINTER's suspicion be sufficient to convict HUNTLEY of driving whilst over the prescribed limit?

A No, suspicion would be enough to prove that HUNTLEY was the driver of a vehicle, but further evidence is required to prove this offence.

B Yes, provided the suspicion was reasonably held.

C No, suspicion would be sufficient to require a breath test, but not to convict HUNTLEY of the offence.

D Yes, suspicion alone would be enough as HUNTLEY is the owner of the car.

Question 5.3

Constable PITROLA was stopped by GRANGER, who had seen a man in a pub earlier, drinking heavily. The man was now sitting in a car outside the pub and GRANGER feared he might drive. As Constable PITROLA approached the car he saw HART sitting in the driver's seat. HART saw the officer and locked all the doors, refusing to open them again.

Would Constable PITROLA have a power to enter the vehicle by force to deal with HART as he is suspected of being unfit to drive through drink or drugs?

A No, GRANGER's suspicion that HART is drunk is not sufficient to provide reasonable suspicion that he is unfit to drive.

B Yes, in order to breathalyse HART, on reasonable suspicion that he is unfit to drive through drink.

C Yes, in order to arrest HART, on reasonable suspicion that he is unfit to drive through drink.

D No, as the power provided under this section is to enter a premises and not a vehicle.

Question 5.4

Constable McDONALD lawfully arrested ROFF for driving while disqualified. On the way to the station, ROFF began acting in a peculiar manner. When they arrived at the custody office, Constable McDONALD could not detect any signs that ROFF had been drinking. A short while later, the officer received information from a colleague that several canisters of butane gas had been found in ROFF's car.

Would Constable McDONALD now be entitled to deal with ROFF for an offence under s. 4 of the Road Traffic Act 1988?

A No, as butane gas is not a 'drug', and it is unlikely that the prosecution will be able show the quantity of it in ROFF's body.

B No, because the officer formed the suspicion that ROFF was intoxicated after he had stopped driving his vehicle.

C Yes, as s. 4 is an indictable offence he can still be dealt with in accordance with the Serious Organised Crime and Police Act 2005.

D Yes, Constable McDONALD has reason to suspect that ROFF has committed an offence under s. 4 of the Act.

Question 5.5

Constable REID stopped ROBERTSON after he had driven through a red traffic light. Constable REID administered a breath test, which was negative. At this point, Constable REID did not form the opinion that ROBERTSON had been drinking and decided to issue a fixed penalty notice. As Constable REID was talking to ROBERTSON, she noticed that his speech was slurred and consequently formed the opinion that he was unfit to drive.

What should Constable REID now do in respect of ROBERTSON, under the Road Traffic Act 1988?

A Wait for 20 minutes, and then ask him to supply another sample of breath.

B Nothing, he has already supplied a sample of breath which was negative.

C The officer should arrest him for an offence contrary to s. 4 (unfit to drive through drink or drugs) to allow prompt and effective investigation of the offence.

D Ask him to supply another sample of breath immediately.

Question 5.6

ROBINSON was involved in an accident when driving home from the pub one evening. The police attended and asked him to provide a sample of breath, which proved to be positive. ROBINSON was charged with the offence, but at his court appearance he pleaded not guilty. His defence was that while he had been in the pub, his friends had bought him alcoholic drinks when he had asked for low alcohol lager.

What is the court likely to decide in respect of the responsibility ROBINSON had to check the contents of the drinks he was given?

A He had some positive duty to check whether the drinks contained alcohol before consuming them.

B He had an absolute duty to check whether the drinks contained alcohol before consuming them.

C He had no duty to check whether the drinks contained alcohol; the fault lay with his friends.

D The fact that he asked for low alcohol lager was sufficient and he had complied with his duty.

Question 5.7

SHELLEY was charged with an offence of being in charge of his motor vehicle on a road, while over the prescribed limit, having been found asleep at the wheel of the vehicle one night. At his court hearing, SHELLEY claimed that he would not have driven the vehicle while he was still unfit to do so.

Who is responsible for proving or disproving SHELLEY's claim, that he was unlikely to drive the vehicle whilst unfit to do so?

A SHELLEY must demonstrate an arguable case that there was no likelihood of his driving whilst unfit to do so.

B The prosecution must demonstrate beyond reasonable doubt that there was a likelihood of SHELLEY driving whilst unfit to do so.

C SHELLEY must demonstrate on the balance of probabilities that there was no likelihood of his driving whilst unfit to do so.

D The prosecution must demonstrate on the balance of probabilities that there was a likelihood of SHELLEY driving whilst unfit to do so.

Question 5.8

BATE appeared in the magistrates' court for an offence under s. 5(1)(b) of the Road Traffic Act 1988, (in charge of a motor vehicle whilst over the prescribed limit). BATE was found in a car holding the ignition keys. In the court case, BATE admitted being over the prescribed limit, but claimed to have only been in the car to recover some documents from the glove compartment, before catching a taxi home. BATE was acquitted on the grounds that magistrates believed that she was not in charge of the vehicle.

Were the magistrates correct to acquit BATE in these circumstances?

A No, BATE has not relied on the defence that she was unlikely to drive the vehicle whilst over the prescribed limit.

B Yes, BATE has produced sufficient evidence that she was not in charge of the vehicle.

C Yes, the prosecution has not produced evidence that BATE was unlikely to drive the vehicle whilst over the prescribed limit.

D Yes, BATE has produced evidence that she was unlikely to drive the vehicle whilst over the prescribed limit.

Question 5.9

Constable SIER was on foot patrol one night, when a vehicle drove past him with a defective headlamp. Constable SIER recognised the driver as being ERSKINE and contacted his control room to ask for the vehicle to be stopped by another officer. Constable WHEELAN was on patrol in uniform about 20 minutes later, when he saw ERSKINE walking along. The vehicle was nowhere in sight.

Would Constable WHEELAN have the power to require a breath test from ERSKINE in these circumstances?

A Yes, but only if he suspects ERSKINE has alcohol in his body.

B Yes, because he has committed a moving traffic offence.

C No, because he did not see ERSKINE driving himself.

D No, because ERSKINE is no longer driving.

Question 5.10

WHEELAN attended a police station to report a crime and spoke to Constable BLOOM. As they were speaking, the officer suspected that WHEELAN may have been drinking and asked whether she had been. WHEELAN stated she had and the officer asked whether or not she had driven to the station. Again, WHEELAN stated she had. Constable BLOOM requested a sample of breath from WHEELAN, which proved to be positive. WHEELAN was charged with the offence, but pleaded not guilty in court, stating that Constable BLOOM should have cautioned her prior to administering the breath test as their conversation constituted an interview.

Is the court likely to accept WHEELAN's defence in these circumstances?

A Yes, as the conversation occurred prior to the breath test, Constable BLOOM had formed the suspicion that WHEELAN had committed an offence and a caution was required.

B No, Constable BLOOM only formed the suspicion an offence had been committed after the breath test was administered, therefore a caution was not required.

C Yes, the questions asked by Constable BLOOM were preliminary to a breath test and designed to establish whether an offence had taken place, therefore a caution was required.

D Yes, Constable BLOOM knew that WHEELAN had been drinking, therefore the question as to whether she had driven there constituted an interview and a caution was required.

Question 5.11

Constable COURT was conducting her first breath test procedure, having stopped KAY, who was driving with a defective light. During the test, Constable COURT failed to hold down a button on the breath test device for the recommended amount of time. However, the reading still showed a positive breath result and Constable COURT arrested KAY.

Has Constable COURT acted correctly in these circumstances?

A Yes, Constable COURT has acted correctly in the circumstances and the arrest is lawful.

B No, the arrest is unlawful, as Constable COURT made a mistake with the procedure.

C No, the arrest is unlawful, but this would not affect the result of the case if KAY provided a positive sample at the station.

D No, the arrest is unlawful, and KAY should have been made to take the test again.

Question 5.12

Constable WU has stopped MULHOLLAND as she was driving her car erratically. The officer could not smell intoxicants on her breath, but she was unsteady on her feet, and she was acting very strangely. Constable WU suspected that she may have taken a drug and that the drug impaired her driving.

Which is true in relation to a preliminary drug test that Constable WU may conduct?

A Constable WU would not have to be in uniform, unlike breath tests in similar circumstances.
B Constable WU could only take the sample at the place where the requirement was made.
C Constable WU could only carry out the test if she has been specially authorised by her Chief Constable.
D Constable WU may, if suitable to the circumstances, take the sample at a police station.

Question 5.13

Constable ZERASCHI was on uniform patrol late at night and stopped a vehicle being driven erratically by SWAN. SWAN became abusive and started swearing at the officer when she asked him if he had been drinking. DC STROUD was passing in a CID car in plain clothes and assisted Constable ZERASCHI. Because of SWAN's attitude and behaviour, DC STROUD asked him to provide a specimen of breath. SWAN continued swearing and being abusive to both officers, ignoring DC STROUD's request, until he was eventually arrested by Constable ZERASCHI for failing to provide a breath test.

Could SWAN be found guilty in these circumstances, of failing to co-operate with a preliminary test, under s. 6(6) of the Road Traffic Act 1988?

A Yes, SWAN could be guilty of the offence in these circumstances.
B No, the officers should have produced the breath test device before making the request under this section.
C No, a person may not be arrested for this offence simply because of his or her attitude when the request was made.
D No, DC STROUD was not in uniform and did not have the authority to make such a request.

Question 5.14

Constable TAYLOR was called to a collision in a shopping centre car park, which was open to the public. SINGH had reversed his car into the path of a dumper truck being driven by WALSH. WALSH was working on an adjacent building site and the dumper truck he was driving was not manufactured for use on roads.

From whom, if anyone, may Constable TAYLOR require a breath test, in these circumstances?

A SINGH only, provided she suspects he has alcohol in his body.
B Neither driver, as the accident did not occur on a road.
C Both drivers, as they have been involved in an accident.
D SINGH only, whether or not she suspects he has alcohol in his body.

Question 5.15

Sergeant ANZANI was off duty, driving home from work and was stopped at a traffic light when a vehicle being driven by PREECE drove into the rear of Sergeant ANZANI's car. Damage was caused to the car, but nobody was injured. Sergeant ANZANI spoke to PREECE and could smell intoxicants. Sergeant ANZANI used a mobile phone to contact the police and Constable NEWMAN, a probationer constable, arrived at the scene. Constable NEWMAN had brought a preliminary breath test device and a hand-held evidential breath test device, but was unsure how to use them. As a result, Sergeant ANZANI asked PREECE to provide a preliminary breath test, which was positive. Sergeant ANZANI arrested PREECE, and asked for an evidential specimen, which also proved to be positive.

Being in plain clothes, was Sergeant ANZANI entitled to conduct the tests, in these circumstances?

A No, as the collision did not involve injury, Sergeant ANZANI was not entitled to make either request.
B No, Sergeant ANZANI was entitled to conduct the preliminary test, but Constable NEWMAN should have conducted the evidential test.
C No, regardless of whether the accident involved injury, Sergeant ANZANI was not entitled to make either request.
D Yes, Sergeant ANZANI was entitled to conduct both tests.

Question 5.16

BALL drove his car into a garden wall and, without stopping, made his way home. He was alone in the car and no other people were involved. Constable DAWE arrived at the scene and, following a PNC check, attended BALL's home address. Constable DAWE found BALL in the front garden of his house and asked him for a sample of breath, as the officer suspected he had been involved in a road traffic accident. BALL refused and was arrested by the officer. BALL refused to go with Constable DAWE and told him to leave his property.

Does Constable DAWE have the power to continue with his arrest now that he has become a trespasser?

A Yes, BALL was arrested before Constable DAWE became a trespasser.

B Yes, Constable DAWE had a power to enter premises, as BALL had been involved in an accident.

C No, the arrest was unlawful, as Constable DAWE was trespassing as soon as he entered the garden.

D No, Constable DAWE has now become a trespasser and must leave the property.

Question 5.17

Constable CAREY was investigating an incident that occurred outside a public house one night. HALL had been found lying in a gutter with blood coming from a head wound. Witnesses had seen PRIOR driving away from the scene, but could not say how HALL had sustained the injury. Constable CAREY attended PRIOR's address and saw a vehicle parked outside matching the description of the one that had driven away from the scene. PRIOR was at home but refused to open the door. Suspecting that an accident involving injury had taken place, Constable CAREY entered the premises by force and administered a breath test, which was positive. The officer then arrested PRIOR and asked for an evidential breath test at the house.

Has Constable CAREY acted correctly in these circumstances?

A No, there was no power of entry as Constable CAREY did not know for certain that an accident involving injury had taken place.

B Yes, Constable CAREY had a reasonable belief that an accident involving injury had taken place and was entitled to remain on the premises to request both specimens.

C Yes, Constable CAREY had a reasonable suspicion that an accident involving injury had taken place and was entitled to remain on the premises to request both specimens.

D No, there is only a power to enter by force and remain on a premises to request a preliminary breath test, not an evidential specimen.

Question 5.18

Constable PENG is trained to conduct preliminary impairment tests. He was called to assist another officer who had stopped a motor vehicle, which was being driven erratically by WENGER. The officer had administered a breath test, which was negative; however, WENGER's behaviour led the officer to believe that he was under the influence of either drink or drugs. On his arrival, Constable PENG gave instructions to WENGER as part of the test, but WENGER was not able to complete the test because of his condition.

Would the officer be able to arrest WENGER now, for failure to complete the impairment test?

A Yes, provided the officer suspects the presence of alcohol or drugs.
B No, as he has not refused to take the impairment test.
C Yes, regardless of whether the officer suspects the presence of alcohol or drugs.
D No, the officer would have to arrest him under s. 4 of the Act.

Question 5.19

Constable ZACHARIA was on mobile patrol and stopped WILSON, who was driving a motor vehicle on a road. Constable ZACHARIA could smell intoxicants on WILSON's breath and requested a preliminary breath test. WILSON refused to supply the test and ran away from Constable ZACHARIA. The officer gave chase and caught WILSON nearby. The officer arrested WILSON for failing to co-operate with the test and called for assistance. Other officers arrived at the scene and one of them had a hand-held evidential breath test device. WILSON agreed to provide an evidential specimen and the result was positive.

Has Constable ZACHARIA acted correctly in these circumstances?

A No, WILSON should have been arrested and taken to the station for failing to co-operate with the first test and an evidential specimen should have been requested there.
B Yes, the officer has acted correctly in these circumstances.
C No, WILSON should have been arrested and returned to where the first request was made and an evidential specimen should have been requested there.
D No, WILSON should not have been arrested for failing to co-operate with the preliminary test; Constable ZACHARIA should have proceeded straight to the request for an evidential specimen.

Question 5.20

Constable WEAR was on mobile patrol and saw BALE driving through a red traffic light. The officer stopped BALE and requested a preliminary breath sample, which proved to be positive. Constable WEAR arrested BALE and then requested two further samples of breath, using a hand-held evidential breath test device. BALE provided two samples; however, the device produced zero readings. Because the preliminary sample had proved positive, Constable WEAR suspected that the hand-held device may be defective. Constable WEAR arrested BALE on suspicion of driving with excess alcohol, based on the preliminary breath sample.

Can BALE be asked to provide two further evidential samples of breath at the police station?

A No, BALE has provided two samples and must now be asked to provide a sample of blood or urine.

B No, a constable may only make this request if there was no device available at the scene. BALE should now be asked to provide a sample of blood or urine.

C Yes, but only if it can be shown that it was impracticable to use a device at the scene

D Yes, the police can request a further two samples of breath at the station under these circumstances alone.

Question 5.21

Constable COLE attended a road traffic accident involving a car which had struck a wall. There were two occupants in the vehicle: PEARSON, the owner, and his friend, STUART. Constable COLE could smell intoxicants on both persons, but neither admitted being the driver of the vehicle at the time of the accident. PEARSON and STUART provided screening samples of breath, which were both positive. They were arrested and taken to the police station.

From whom, if either, could a specimen of breath for analysis be requested, under s. 7 of the Road Traffic Act 1988 (provision of specimens for analysis)?

A Both, provided it is believed one of them was driving.

B PEARSON only, as the owner of the vehicle.

C Both, regardless of who was suspected to be the driver.

D Neither, Constable COLE should not have breathalysed both persons.

Question 5.22

Sergeant SWEENEY was conducting the station breath test procedure in relation to DENNY. DENNY provided one specimen of breath, which was over the prescribed limit. However, before he could provide a second specimen, the machine malfunctioned and Sergeant SWEENEY was unable to complete the procedure.

What action should Sergeant SWEENEY have taken in order to complete the station procedure?

A Request that DENNY provides a sample of blood or urine, and use that reading, together with the breath test reading as evidence.

B Charge DENNY with driving with excess alcohol, using the one reading as evidence that he was over the limit.

C The only option available to Sergeant SWEENEY is to request that DENNY provides a sample of blood to replace the reading.

D Sergeant SWEENEY may transfer DENNY to another station if there is another machine available.

Question 5.23

Section 7 of the Road Traffic Act 1988 deals with the provision of specimens for analysis.

In which of the scenarios below, where the defendant has been arrested for providing a positive roadside breath test, will the custody officer have acted *incorrectly* in respect of a requirement made under s. 7?

A The custody officer has requested a blood sample from THYNNE instead of two specimens of breath because the breath test machine is defective.

B The custody officer has required BERRY to provide a blood sample for medical reasons, and has transferred him to another station, where a doctor is available.

C The custody officer has requested a blood sample from KELLIHER, as there is no trained officer available to take specimens of breath.

D A blood sample was obtained from BADKIN; however, the custody officer reverted to a previously obtained breath sample.

Question 5.24

COLE was arrested for failing to provide a roadside breath test. On his arrival at the police station, COLE provided two samples of breath. Both readings were very low. However, the custody officer, Sergeant WONG, believed that COLE may have taken drugs as he was exhibiting similar behaviour to a drunken person.

What would be the correct course of action for Sergeant WONG to take in these circumstances?

A Consult a doctor, who must confirm in writing that COLE's behaviour is due to his taking drugs and then request a sample of blood or urine.

B Request a blood or urine sample from COLE and then call a doctor to take either the blood sample or urine sample.

C Consult a doctor, who must confirm verbally that COLE's behaviour is due to his taking drugs and then request a sample of blood or urine.

D Request a blood or urine sample from COLE and then call a doctor to take the sample, if it is blood, or take the sample himself if it is urine.

Question 5.25

Constable HAYES conducted the station breath test procedure for BOBIN. The lowest reading was 49 microgrammes of alcohol in 100 millilitres of breath and BOBIN elected to replace the samples. Constable HAYES decided that BOBIN should provide a specimen of blood. However, BOBIN failed to provide a specimen and was charged with the offence. BOBIN pleaded not guilty in court, citing that Constable HAYES had failed to issue a warning under s. 7(7) of the Road Traffic Act 1988 (failure to provide the specimen may render a person liable to prosecution).

If Constable HAYES did fail to issue a warning, would BOBIN's defence be successful?

A No, the warning was not required in these circumstances.

B Yes, the warning should have been given by the person conducting the procedure.

C Yes, the warning should have been given by a constable, not necessarily the person conducting the procedure.

D No, the warning under s. 7(7) only relates to provisions of specimens of breath.

Question 5.26

Constable BERKIN was conducting the station breath test procedure for CAREY. The lowest reading was 48 microgrammes of alcohol in 100 millilitres of breath and CAREY elected to replace the samples. Constable BERKIN decided that CAREY should provide a specimen of blood, but she stated it was against her religion to provide blood, and that on medical grounds she would prefer to provide urine. Constable BERKIN did not believe the medical grounds were valid and asked VORIN, a registered health care professional to attend the station to take the sample.

Is VORIN authorised to make the decision that CAREY should continue to provide a specimen of blood under s. 7(4) of the Road Traffic Act 1988, in these circumstances?

A No, only a medical practitioner can make this decision in these circumstances.

B Yes, provided a medical practitioner has been consulted first.

C Yes, provided a medical practitioner has not declared that there is a medical reason preventing CAREY from providing the specimen.

D No, the decision as to whether the specimen should be blood or urine is entirely Constable BERKIN's.

Question 5.27

Constable DAMON was on mobile patrol and stopped a vehicle being driven by SHALKE. Constable DAMON suspected that SHALKE had been drinking and requested a preliminary breath test and the test proved positive. Constable DAMON arrested SHALKE and requested two further samples of breath, using a hand-held evidential breath test device. SHALKE provided the samples and the lowest reading was 49 microgrammes of alcohol in 100 millilitres of breath. Constable DAMON informed SHALKE that the breath sample could be replaced by a sample of blood or urine and SHALKE requested this course of action.

What action should Constable DAMON take now?

A SHALKE may now be arrested and taken to a police station for a blood or urine sample to be obtained.

B SHALKE should now be taken to a police station to obtain two further samples of breath.

C SHALKE may be asked to attend a police station voluntarily but if SHALKE refuses, the lowest reading should be used and there is no power of arrest.

D SHALKE must now be arrested and taken to a police station for a blood or urine sample to be obtained.

Question 5.28

KHAN has provided two specimens of breath during the station breath test procedure, the readings being 49 and 50 respectively. Sergeant WILSON informed KHAN that he could replace the samples with blood or urine. KHAN stated that he would prefer not to give blood, as he had a fear of needles. Sergeant WILSON has been informed that a doctor is available by telephone only and will not attend immediately.

What action should Sergeant WILSON now take in respect of KHAN?

A Speak to the doctor on the telephone and proceed as advised by him or her.

B Request a sample of blood if necessary; a fear of needles is not a medical reason for not giving blood.

C Take a sample of urine from KHAN, as the choice is his as to which sample may be taken.

D Wait until the doctor arrives and proceed as advised by him or her; such advice may not be taken by telephone.

Question 5.29

JONES was arrested following a positive roadside breath test and taken to a police station. He provided a further two samples of breath, the readings being 48 and 47 respectively. JONES later provided a specimen of blood, which was divided and a portion given to him. The arresting officer received notification a few weeks later that an error had occurred with the sample forwarded for analysis, and that it could not be used in evidence.

What options are now open to the arresting officer, in order to proceed against JONES for the offence of driving with excess alcohol?

A Both breath specimens may be used as evidence to prosecute JONES for the offence.

B JONES may be prosecuted, using the lower reading as evidence.

C JONES may not be prosecuted in these circumstances; the case must be dismissed.

D The lower reading may be used as evidence, and the court must decide on the balance of probabilities if he is guilty.

Question 5.30

Sergeant DONELLY was conducting the station breath test procedure for BEECH, who had provided one sample of breath. However, BEECH stated that he was tired, and fell asleep before providing a second sample. Sergeant DONELLY tried to wake BEECH, without success, and in the end placed him in a cell. BEECH was later charged with driving with excess alcohol, based on the reading provided, which was 150 microgrammes of alcohol in 100 millilitres of breath.

Has Sergeant DONELLY acted correctly in these circumstances?

A Yes, Sergeant DONELLY has acted correctly in these circumstances as BEECH has driven with excess alcohol.

B No, BEECH should have been charged with failing to provide a sample, but his drunken condition may provide a defence.

C No, BEECH should have been given the opportunity to provide a sample of blood or urine when he was sober enough.

D No, BEECH should have been charged with failing to provide a sample and would have no defence arising from his drunken condition.

Question 5.31

Constable BRUNO was conducting the station breath test procedure for COULTER, who had been arrested for a positive preliminary breath test. Before applying the test, Constable BRUNO asked if COULTER had eaten anything recently. COULTER admitted having eaten a mint, but the officer continued with the procedure, asking COULTER to supply two samples of breath. COULTER refused to supply the samples and was charged with failing to co-operate with the procedure. At court, COULTER pleaded not guilty citing that Constable BRUNO had failed to follow procedures by not waiting 20 minutes after asking the question in respect of the food. When questioned in court, Constable BRUNO admitted to being unaware of police guidelines to wait 20 minutes.

Would Constable BRUNO's failure to comply with guidelines provide COULTER with a defence to the charge, in these circumstances?

A No, because Constable BRUNO was unaware of police guidelines.

B Yes, the 20-minute waiting period is mandatory and should have been followed.

C No, COULTER failed to provide a sample and the reliability of a test was not compromised.

D Yes, regardless of whether COULTER failed to provide a sample.

Question 5.32

WRIGHT is appearing in court, having been charged with an offence under s. 5(1)(a) of the Road Traffic Act 1988 (over the prescribed limit). WRIGHT had provided two samples of breath and the lowest reading was 47 microgrammes of alcohol in 100 millilitres of breath. WRIGHT later replaced the breath samples with a specimen of blood. The prosecution is relying on the evidence of the blood specimen, which showed that the proportion of alcohol in WRIGHT's body exceeded the prescribed limit.

Which of the following statements is correct, in respect of whether the machine used to obtain the breath samples, was both reliable and of an approved type?

A The prosecution must show that the device was reliable and of an approved type.

B There is no requirement to show the device was of an approved type or that it was reliable, as the prosecution is not relying on the samples of breath.

C The prosecution must show the device is of an approved type; the defence should introduce evidence, if they felt the device was unreliable.

D The prosecution must show the device is of an approved type; there is no requirement to show the device was reliable, as they are not relying on the samples of breath.

Question 5.33

MILLARD was charged with causing death by careless driving, whilst unfit to drive through drugs. MILLARD proposed to introduce evidence in court to prove that she had not been under the influence of drugs at the time of the alleged offence. MILLARD contested that she had taken drugs after she had ceased to drive her car, and was no longer in charge of it.

What effect will this have on the court's ability to make an assumption, under s. 15 of the Road Traffic Offenders Act 1988, that the proportion of drugs in MILLARD's body was the same at the time of the accident as when she later provided the sample?

A The court will take into account any sample provided by MILLARD only if the prosecution can discredit her evidence.

B None, the court would not have been able to make that assumption as MILLARD was not under the influence of alcohol.

C None, the assumption under s. 15 does not apply to the offence that MILLARD is alleged to have committed.

D None, only the prosecution may introduce such evidence and since they have not, the court must take into account the sample.

Question 5.34

PC ELGAR attempted to stop DRUMMOND, who was driving a motor vehicle on a road. DRUMMOND failed to stop for the officer and was lost in traffic. PC ELGAR attended DRUMMOND's house an hour later after conducting a Police National Computer (PNC) check. DRUMMOND answered the door and the officer detected the smell of intoxicants on his breath. DRUMMOND provided Constable ELGAR with a specimen of breath, which was positive. Further evidential samples were taken from DRUMMOND, which exceeded the prescribed limit. DRUMMOND later claimed in court that he had drunk alcohol between the time he had stopped driving and provided the sample of breath, which caused his reading to be over the prescribed limit.

Which of the following statements is correct, in relation to the burden of proof in such cases?

A DRUMMOND will need to show that on the balance of probabilities, he was not over the limit when he drove.

B The prosecution will need to show beyond reasonable doubt that DRUMMOND was over the limit when he drove.

C DRUMMOND will need to show that on the balance of probabilities, he was not over the limit when he drove — the prosecution must then show beyond reasonable doubt that he was.

D The prosecution will need to show beyond reasonable doubt that DRUMMOND was over the limit when he drove — DRUMMOND will then need to show that on the balance of probabilities he was not.

Question 5.35

PREEDEY is appearing in court having been charged with driving whilst over the limit. PREEDEY provided a specimen of blood whilst in detention which, when examined, showed evidence that the proportion of alcohol in it exceeded the prescribed limit. However, PREEDEY is pleading not guilty on the grounds that she was not supplied with part of the specimen by the police.

Which of the following statements is correct, in relation to whether or not the police should have supplied PREEDEY with part of the specimen of blood?

A PREEDEY should have been informed of her right to be supplied with part of the specimen and it should have been given to her.

B PREEDEY should have been informed of her right to be supplied with part of the specimen, but it should only have been given to her if she requested it.

C There was no statutory requirement to inform PREEDEY of her right to be supplied with part of the specimen, or to supply it to her unless she requested it.

D There was no statutory requirement to inform PREEDEY of her right to be supplied with part of the specimen, but if she did not ask for it, it should have been offered to her.

Question 5.36

GOUGH was in custody for driving whilst over the limit and has provided a specimen of blood for analysis. Section 15(5) of the Road Traffic Offenders Act 1988, deals with the provision of part of the specimen to GOUGH after it has been taken.

In relation to the provision of such a sample, which of the following statements is correct?

A It must be divided at the time it was taken, in GOUGH's presence and given to GOUGH immediately afterwards.

B It must be divided at the time it was taken, but not necessarily in GOUGH's presence and given to GOUGH within a reasonable time.

C It must be divided at the time it was taken or as soon as practicable afterwards, in GOUGH's presence and given to GOUGH within a reasonable time.

D It must be divided at the time it was taken but not necessarily in GOUGH's presence, but it must be given to GOUGH immediately afterwards.

Question 5.37

PEARCE has been charged with an offence of driving with excess alcohol (under s. 5 of the Road Traffic Act 1988) and is still in custody. Sergeant REVERS is considering whether or not to detain PEARCE at the custody office, because the lowest reading of the sample provided by PEARCE was 130 microgrammes of alcohol in 100 millilitres of breath.

What matters should Sergeant REVERS take into consideration, before detaining PEARCE under s. 10(1) of the Road Traffic Act 1988?

A Sergeant REVERS has a statutory power to confiscate PEARCE's car keys under this subsection, to prevent her from committing an offence under s. 5 or s. 4 of the Act.

B Sergeant REVERS has a statutory power to detain PEARCE until she has provided a negative screening test, to prevent her from committing an offence under s. 5 or s. 4 of the Act.

C PEARCE may be detained, provided Sergeant REVERS has reasonable grounds to believe she will not commit an offence under s. 5 or s. 4 if she were to drive a motor vehicle on a road.

D PEARCE may be detained, provided Sergeant REVERS has reasonable grounds to believe she will not commit an offence under s. 5 or s. 4 if she were to drive a mechanically propelled vehicle on a road.

Question 5.38

NEWMAN is in custody and is suspected of being unfit to drive through taking drugs. NEWMAN has provided a specimen of blood, which the custody officer, Sergeant BURKE, intends to submit for analysis. NEWMAN will not be charged until the results of the analysis are known and, therefore, Sergeant BURKE intends to release him on bail for the period. However, NEWMAN has stated his intention to drive when released. Sergeant BURKE suspects that NEWMAN would still be unfit if he were to drive a motor vehicle on a road.

What does s. 10 of the Road Traffic Act 1988 say, in relation to the advice Sergeant BURKE should seek, before detaining NEWMAN further until he is fit to drive a motor vehicle on a road?

A Sergeant BURKE may make this decision herself; she does not need to seek advice from anyone.

B Sergeant BURKE may seek advice from a doctor, and must act on any advice given.

C Sergeant BURKE may not detain NEWMAN under this section, as he has not been charged or reported for an offence.

D Sergeant BURKE must seek advice from a doctor, and must act on any advice given.

Question 5.39

ASKEW was involved in a road traffic accident during which she received head injuries, and was taken to hospital. The officer dealing with the accident, Constable LEE, was told by witnesses that ASKEW's driving was erratic immediately prior to the accident. Constable LEE attended the hospital to interview ASKEW and require her to provide a sample of breath. On his arrival, Constable LEE was told that ASKEW was unconscious due to her injuries. Constable LEE considered that a sample of blood should be taken from ASKEW without her permission.

Who would be able to take such a sample from ASKEW, under s. 7A of the Road Traffic Act 1988?

A A police medical practitioner or the medical practitioner in charge of the patient.

B A police medical practitioner or any other medical practitioner, but not the one in charge of the patient.

C A police medical practitioner only.

D A police medical practitioner, the medical practitioner in charge of the patient or a registered health care professional.

Question 5.40

WEBBER was at a hospital, having been involved in a road traffic accident. Having consulted with WEBBER's doctor, Constable O'SHEA required WEBBER to provide a specimen of breath, but she refused. Constable O'SHEA arrested WEBBER for failing to provide a specimen. After further consultation with the doctor, Constable O'SHEA asked WEBBER to supply a specimen of blood.

Has Constable O'SHEA complied with the requirements of s. 9 of the Road Traffic Act 1988?

A No, because WEBBER was under arrest, the request for blood should have been made at a police station.

B No, he should not have arrested WEBBER while she was still a patient at the hospital.

C Yes, as the doctor has agreed to both specimens being requested, he has complied with the Act.

D Yes, but there was no need to ask permission on the second occasion, as permission had already been granted.

Question 5.41

Section 156 of the Licensing Act 2003 makes it an offence to sell by retail alcohol on or from a vehicle.

Which of the following would be a vehicle subject to this legislation?

A Only a vehicle subject to Public Service Vehicle regulations.

B Any vehicle designed to carry more than 8 passengers.

C Any vehicle designed to carry more than 16 passengers.

D Any vehicle intended for use on a road.

Question 5.42

There are regulations governing the sale of alcohol at certain 'restricted premises'.

Which of the following is true in relation to these regulations?

A They apply to a garage that repairs and changes tyres on motor vehicles.

B They apply to a garage that repairs motor vehicles but only if it also sells petrol/derv.

C They only apply to a garage that sells petrol/derv.

D The restriction specifically does not apply to any part of a motorway service area.

ANSWERS

Answer 5.1

Answer **B** — The High Risk Offender Scheme is designed to emphasise the safety considerations in driving while unfit or over the prescribed limit.

The scheme generally applies to offenders who are convicted of the relevant offences and at the time were more than two and a half times over the prescribed limit, or for whom the conviction is their second (or more) in ten years. Answers C and D are therefore incorrect.

Although the level of alcohol may be relevant information, it is not relevant in the present case, because GUILLAM's case attracts the scheme because it is the second conviction in 10 years. Answer A is therefore incorrect.

Road Policing, para. 3.5.1

Answer 5.2

Answer **C** — Under s. 6(3) of the Road Traffic Act 1988, if a constable reasonably suspects that the person has been driving, attempting to drive or is in charge of a motor vehicle on a road or other public place while having alcohol or a drug in his body or while unfit to drive because of a drug, and the person still has alcohol or a drug in his body or is still under the influence of a drug, he or she may require a person to co-operate with any one or more preliminary tests administered to the person by that constable or another constable.

However, although reasonable suspicion may be sufficient to require a breath sample, it would not be enough to rely on mere suspicion that the defendant had been driving prior to the administration of the test, and the officer would have to prove that the defendant had been driving before he or she could be convicted (see *R (on the application of Huntley)* v *DPP* [2004] EWHC 870). Answer A is therefore incorrect.

This is true whether or not the suspicion was reasonably held by the officer, even if it could be shown that the suspect was the owner of the car and was found nearby (although this would be strong circumstantial evidence and would benefit the case if other evidence were uncovered, such as witness substantiation). Answers B and D are therefore incorrect.

Road Policing, paras 3.5.2, 3.5.4, 3.1.3.4

Answer 5.3

Answer **C** — The power to arrest and deal with persons unfit through drink/drugs has been amended by the Serious Organised Crime and Police Act 2005. The power to arrest previously granted by s. 4(6) of the Road Traffic Act 1988 has been repealed, as has the power of entry given by s. 4(7).

Section 17(1) of the Police and Criminal Evidence Act 1984 now states:

> (1) Subject to the following provisions of this section, and without prejudice to any other enactment, a constable may enter and search any premises for the purpose —
>
> (c) of arresting a person for an offence under —
>
> (iiia) section 4 (driving etc when under influence of drink or drugs) or 163 (failure to stop when required to do so by constable in uniform) of the Road Traffic Act 1988;

So there still remains power to enter to arrest, provided that such arrest is necessary under s. 100 of the Serious Organised Crime and Police Act 2005 (the replacement of s. 24 of the Police and Criminal Evidence Act 1984). There is no power of entry to breathalyse; answer B is therefore incorrect. Premises is not defined, but would include vehicles; answer D is therefore incorrect.

Evidence of impairment must be produced by the prosecution, and that evidence may be provided by a 'lay' witness, provided that witness is not required to give expert testimony or to comment on the defendant's ability to drive (*R* v *Lanfear* [1968] 2 QB 77). Answer A is therefore incorrect.

Road Policing, para. 3.5.2.1

Answer 5.4

Answer **D** — 'Drugs' for the purpose of s. 4 of the Road Traffic Act 1988 will include any intoxicant other than alcohol (s. 11), and will include *toluene* found in some glues (*Bradford* v *Wilson* (1983) 78 Cr App R 77). As the effects of butane gas can be 'intoxicating', this will be included as an intoxicant. Unlike offences under s. 5, it is not necessary under s. 4 to show what quantity of alcohol or drug the defendant had in his or her system to convict of the offence. Answer A is therefore incorrect.

The suspicion need not be formed while the defendant is driving and can become apparent after he or she has been stopped or spoken to for some other reason (*R* v *Roff* [1976] RTR 7). Answer B is therefore incorrect.

Section 4 is not an indictable offence and in any case the Serious Organised Crime and Police Act 2005 only repealed powers in relation to s. 4, it did not add to them; answer C is therefore incorrect.

Road Policing, para. 3.5.2.1

Answer 5.5

Answer **C** — Section 4 of the Road Traffic Act 1988, states:

(1) A person who, when driving or attempting to drive a mechanically propelled vehicle on a road or other public place, is unfit to drive through drink or drugs is guilty of an offence.

(2) Without prejudice to subsection (1) above, a person who, when in charge of a mechanically propelled vehicle which is on a road or other public place, is unfit to drive through drink or drugs is guilty of an offence.

The circumstances in the question mirror those in the case of *DPP* v *Robertson* [2002] RTR 383. In this case, the Administrative Court decided that even though the driver had provided a negative screening test, he was seen moments later staggering in a way which gave rise to a suspicion of unfitness. In such a case, s. 4 of the Act could still be used to show that the person was unfit to drive. Although the Serious Organised Crime and Police Act 2005 repealed the statutory power of arrest given by s. 4(6) of the 1988 Act, under s. 24 of the Police and Criminal Evidence Act 1984 (as amended by s. 110 of the 2005 Act) a person can be arrested for any offence, provided that it is necessary within the criteria set out in s. 24(5) of the Police and Criminal Evidence Act 1984. One of those being to allow the prompt and effective investigation of the offence or of the conduct of the person in question, in this case there could be no other way to deal with this offence. Answers A, B and D are therefore incorrect.

Road Policing, paras 3.5.2, 3.5.2.1

Answer 5.6

Answer **A** — The facts in this question are taken from *Robinson* v *DPP* [2003] EWHC 2718. In that case, the Divisional Court held that a person is under *some positive duty* to check whether drinks contained alcohol before consuming them, if the person intends to drive afterwards. Answers B, C and D are therefore incorrect.

Road Policing, para. 3.5.3

Answer 5.7

Answer **A** — Section 5(2) of the Road Traffic Act 1988 provides a defence for a person charged with an offence under s. 5(1)(b) (in charge of a motor vehicle whilst over the prescribed limit), provided there was no likelihood of him or her driving the vehicle whilst unfit.

The situation was examined in the Divisional Court, in the case of *Sheldrake* v *DPP* [2003] 2 All ER 497. The defendant claimed that the application of s. 5(2) above was contrary to Art. 6(2) of the European Convention on Human Rights (presumption of innocence). The court held that s. 5(2) did not breach Article 6(2), and that a person charged with an offence under s. 5(1)(b) above must demonstrate from the evidence an arguable case that there was no likelihood of him driving whilst unfit to do so. Answer C is therefore incorrect.

The prosecution do have a responsibility under s. 5(2) above to show beyond reasonable doubt that there was a likelihood of the defendant driving, but *only if* the defendant has first presented a successful argument as referred to above. Since the initial responsibility lies with the defendant, answers B and D are incorrect.

The above case came before the House of Lords as *Attorney General's Reference (No. 4 of 2002) Sheldrake* v *DPP* [2004] UKHL 43. There it was held that, although s. 5(2) did in fact infringe the presumption of innocence under Article 6, the burden placed on the defendant was reasonable because it was in pursuance of a legitimate aim. The likelihood of the defendant's driving was so closely linked to his or her own knowledge at the relevant time that it made it much more appropriate for the defendant to prove — on the balance of probabilities — that he or she would not have been likely to drive (as opposed to the prosecution being required to prove the opposite beyond reasonable doubt).

Road Policing, para. 3.5.3.1

Answer 5.8

Answer **A** — The circumstances in the question are similar to those in case of *Crown Prosecution Service* v *Bate* [2004] EWHC 2811. In that case the defendant had been found in a car with the keys to the ignition in his hand. Following a positive breath test, he appeared at court charged under s. 5(1)(b). The defendant argued that he had only been in the car for the purpose of retrieving a disabled permit before ringing his wife to arrange a taxi for him to get home. The magistrates' court accepted this account and the defendant was acquitted.

The CPS appealed to the Divisional Court, which held that the defendant *had* been 'in charge' of the vehicle at the time of the offence. Answer B is incorrect, because the person in the question *was* in charge of the vehicle.

The remaining question was whether or not the defendant was likely to drive the vehicle whilst still being over the prescribed limit. Section 5(2) of the Act places the burden firmly on the defendant to show that he/she was unlikely to drive in that state (and not the prosecution, therefore, answer C is therefore incorrect).

However, in *Bate*, the Court held that the likelihood of the defendant's driving the vehicle while still over the limit was only relevant if and when he/she raised the statutory defence. It was held that Bate had not, in fact, relied on s. 5(2) above, because he had not actually produced evidence that he was unlikely to drive the vehicle, (answer D is therefore incorrect). Had Bate done so, this evidence could have been considered by the Court and the usual considerations with regard to standards of proof would then apply.

Road Policing, para. 3.5.3.1

Answer 5.9

Answer **B** — Sections 6(4)(a)–(b) of the Road Traffic Act 1988 state that a preliminary breath test may be required if a constable reasonably suspects that the person is or has been driving or attempting to drive, or is or has been in charge of a motor vehicle on a road or other public place and has committed a traffic offence while the vehicle was in motion. Answer D is incorrect, as the test may be required as the driver *was* driving while committing a moving traffic offence.

Where the person is suspected of committing an offence while the vehicle was in motion, there is no requirement for the officer to suspect that he or she has alcohol in his or her body, or still has alcohol in his or her body when making the request (this is in contrast to the requirements under s. 6(2) and (3) of the 1988 Act of driving/attempting to drive or being in charge). Answer A is therefore incorrect.

One officer's 'reasonable cause to suspect' may arise from the observations of another officer (*Erskine* v *Hollin* [1971] RTR 199). Answer C is therefore incorrect.

Road Policing, paras 3.5.4, 3.5.4.1

Answer 5.10

Answer **B** — The facts in the question are similar to the case of *Ridehalgh* v *DPP* [2005] RTR 26. In this case, the defendant (a police officer) argued that the questions asked prior to the breath test procedure constituted an interview and as he had not been cautioned, Code C, paras. 10.1 and 11.1(A) of the Codes of Practice had been breached. It was held that no interview had taken place and that there had been no breach of Code C. It was held that the questions regarding driving and whether he had been drinking first were merely preliminary and had been made with the intention of finding the possibility of whether an offence had been committed. On appeal the Divisional Court held that a necessary precondition of the giving of a caution was that there had to be grounds for the suspicion of a criminal offence and that the magistrates were correct. The police officers merely suspected that the defendant had been drinking alcohol; they had no indication as to how much alcohol had been consumed, or whether he had actually driven. The ruling followed an earlier, similar decision in the case of *Whelehan* v *DPP* [1995] RTR 177. Answers A, C and D are therefore incorrect.

Road Policing, para. 3.5.4.1

Answer 5.11

Answer **A** — It has been held that where a constable innocently fails to follow the manufacturer's instructions, it will not render the test nor any subsequent arrest unlawful (*DPP* v *Kay* [1999] RTR 109). Answer B is therefore incorrect. Answer C is also incorrect, as the arrest was not unlawful.

In addition to the case of *Kay* above, it was decided in *DPP* v *Carey* [1969] 3 All ER 1662, that failing to comply with the manufacturer's instructions on the use of an approved device will mean that the person *has not provided* a preliminary breath test and *may* be asked to provide another; refusing to do so will be an offence. Answer D is incorrect, as the case is not the authority for the view that a person *must* be made to take another test. Since the purpose of the test is to indicate whether there is a *likelihood* of an offence being committed, an arrest in these circumstances is appropriate, as the test did show a positive result.

Road Policing, para. 3.5.4.2

Answer 5.12

Answer **D** — The Road Traffic Act 1988, s. 6C states:

(1) A preliminary drug test is a procedure by which a specimen of sweat or saliva is —
- (a) obtained, and
- (b) used for the purpose of obtaining, by means of a device of a type approved by the Secretary of State, an indication whether the person to whom the test is administered has a drug in his body.

(2) A preliminary drug test may be administered —
 (a) at or near the place where the requirement to co-operate with the test is imposed, or
 (b) if the constable who imposes the requirement thinks it expedient, at a police station specified by him...

As the test can be carried out at a police station answer B is incorrect.

All the procedures under s. 6, i.e. preliminary breath test, preliminary impairment test and preliminary drug test, must be administered by a constable only if they are in uniform (s. 6(7)). Answer A is therefore incorrect.

A preliminary impairment test under s. 6B is a completely different procedure from the other two and involves an appropriately trained and authorised police officer observing the person performing specified tasks. This special authorisation does not extend to s. 6C; therefore answer C is incorrect.

Road Policing, para. 3.5.4.2

Answer 5.13

Answer **A** — Under s. 6(6) of the Road Traffic Act 1988, a person commits an offence if without reasonable excuse he or she fails to co-operate with a preliminary test in pursuance of a requirement imposed under this section.

Under s. 6(7) of the Act, the officer administering the breath test must be in uniform; however, there is no need for the officer making the requirement to be in uniform. Answer D is therefore incorrect.

A person's attitude and conduct after being required to give a specimen under s. 6A may be sufficient to make out an offence under s. 6(6), and the evidence of the officer witnessing the conduct may suffice as proof that it amounted to a failure or refusal, (see *DPP* v *Swan* [2004] EWHC 2432). Answer C is therefore incorrect. Also, according to the ruling in *Swan*, if a person does something which amounts to a refusal to provide a preliminary breath test, the offence will be made out even though the officer did not produce a device for doing so. Answer B is therefore incorrect.

Road Policing, paras 3.5.4.2, 3.5.4.4

Answer 5.14

Answer **D** — The power to conduct a breath test under s. 6(5) of the Road Traffic Act 1988 applies where an accident has occurred owing to the presence of a motor vehicle on a road or public place. Since Walsh was driving a mechanically propelled vehicle and not a motor vehicle, there is no power to request a breath test from him. Answer C is therefore incorrect. As s. 6 applies to accidents that occur in a public place as well as on a road, answer B is also incorrect.

There is no need for the officer making the enquiry to suspect or believe that the driver has been drinking, nor that he has committed an offence in order to require a breath test following an accident. Answer A is therefore incorrect.

Road Policing, para. 3.5.4.3

Answer 5.15

Answer **D** — Section 6(5) of the Road Traffic Act 1988 provides that following an accident involving a motor vehicle on a road, a constable may require the driver to provide a specimen of breath for a breath test. The section does not require the officer to be in uniform. Answer C is therefore incorrect. There is no requirement for an injury to have occurred for the power to be used under this section — answer A is therefore incorrect.

The Serious Organised Crime and Police Act 2005 has amended s. 6 of the Road Traffic Act 1988, so as to permit police to carry out an evidential breath test not only at a police station, but also at a hospital, or at or near a place (such as the roadside) where a preliminary breath test has been administered. Where a constable has imposed a requirement to co-operate with a preliminary breath test under s. 6(5) above, he or she may also require an evidential breath specimen under s.7(2)(c), at or near the place where the preliminary breath test has been administered. A requirement under s. 7(2)(c) may not be made unless the constable is in uniform, or the constable has imposed a requirement to co-operate with a relevant breath test under s. 6(5) of the Act (which is the case in this question). Answer B is therefore incorrect.

Road Policing, paras 3.5.4.3, 3.5.5.1

Answer 5.16

Answer **A** — Generally, where an officer is trespassing on a defendant's property, he or she is not entitled to require a breath test (*R* v *Fox* [1986] AC 281). Also, if officers are trespassing, any subsequent arrest made by them is unlawful (*Clowser* v *Chaplin* [1981] RTR 317). However, any requirement for a sample of breath properly made and any subsequent arrest remains lawful until the officer becomes a trespasser.

A police officer, like any other citizen, has an implied licence to go on to certain parts of property (which might include a garden), unless and until that licence is withdrawn. It is when the licence is withdrawn that the officer may become a trespasser. Therefore, if a police officer is on the defendant's property and has not been told to leave, any requirement for a breath test and subsequent arrest is lawful (*Pamplin* v *Fraser* [1981] RTR 494). This would still be the case even if the licence were withdrawn later. Answer D is therefore incorrect.

In the scenario given, the officer was not a trespasser until the defendant told him to leave the garden. Answer C is therefore incorrect.

Constable DAWE has no statutory power to enter the premises under s. 6E of the Road Traffic Act 1988, as this section only affords a power of entry following an accident involving injury to a person other than the driver. Answer B is incorrect as the scenario did not involve an injury.

Road Policing, para. 3.5.4.5

Answer 5.17

Answer **A** — Under s. 6E(1)(a) of the Road Traffic Act 1988, a constable may enter any place using reasonable force for the purpose of requesting a preliminary breath test following an accident involving injury. Before the power is used, there are four criteria that must apply. The officer must:

- know that an accident has taken place (mere suspicion is not enough);
- have reasonable cause to believe that the person had been driving or attempting to drive, or had been in charge of the vehicle (mere suspicion is not enough);
- have reasonable cause to suspect that the accident involved injury to another person (here suspicion is enough); and
- have reasonable cause to suspect that the person he or she is seeking is in the place to be entered (again suspicion is enough).

Since Constable CAREY did not know for certain that an accident had taken place, there was no power to enter the premises. Answers B and C are therefore incorrect.

Where a constable imposes a requirement to co-operate with a preliminary breath test at any place, he or she is entitled to remain at or near the place in order to impose on the person an evidential specimen under s. 7 (s. 7(2C)). Answer D is therefore incorrect.

Road Policing, paras 3.5.4.5, 3.5.4.6

Answer 5.18

Answer **A** — Under s. 6B of the Road Traffic Act 1988, an appropriately trained officer has the power to require the driver of a motor vehicle on a road or public place to submit to a preliminary impairment test, to observe the driver's behaviour. Such observations may be used as evidence in any subsequent court cases — but will not provide absolute proof of a person's guilt.

A person who fails to co-operate with a preliminary impairment test commits an offence under s. 6(6) of the Act. A person does not co-operate unless his or her cooperation is sufficient to allow the test to be carried out (s. 11(3)). In the question, the driver's behaviour meant that the test could not be carried out, even though he did not refuse to take it. Answer B is therefore incorrect.

A constable may arrest a person who has failed to co-operate with a test under this section, *provided* the constable reasonably suspects that the person has alcohol or drugs in his or her body, or is under the influence of drugs (s. 6D(2)). Answers C and D are therefore incorrect.

Road Policing, paras 3.5.4.2, 3.5.4.4, 3.5.4.7

Answer 5.19

Answer **B** — Under s. 6D(2) of the Road Traffic Act 1988, a constable may arrest without warrant any person who fails to co-operate with a preliminary test in pursuance with a requirement imposed under s. 6 of the Act and the constable reasonably suspects that the person has alcohol or a drug in his or her body or is under the influence of a drug (the officer suspected that WILSON had been drinking and therefore has complied with this section).

Section 7 of the Road Traffic Act 1988 (the obtaining of evidential samples) has been amended by the Serious Organised Crime and Police Act 2005 so as to permit police to carry out an evidential breath test not only at a police station, but also at a hospital, or at or near a place (such as the roadside) where a preliminary breath test has been administered. Section 6D(2A) states that a person arrested under s. 6D(2) above may, instead of being taken to a police station, be detained at or near the place where the preliminary test was, or would have been, administered, with a view to imposing on him or her there a requirement under s. 7. Answers A and C are therefore incorrect.

The power to request an evidential test at the scene under s. 7 does not negate the powers of arrest already in place under s. 6D(2). Therefore, there was nothing preventing the officer from arresting the suspect for a failure to co-operate with the initial request and proceeding with the request for an evidential sample at or near the scene. Answer D is incorrect.

Road Policing, para. 3.5.4.7

Answer 5.20

Answer **D** — Section 7 of the Road Traffic Act 1988 (the obtaining of evidential samples) has been amended by the Serious Organised Crime and Police Act 2005 so as to permit police to carry out an evidential breath test not only at a police station, but also at a hospital, or at or near a place (such as the roadside) where a preliminary breath test has been administered. Section 7(2D) of the Road Traffic Act 1988 states that if a requirement is made under s. 7(1)(a) at a place other than a police station, such a requirement may subsequently be made at a police station if (but only if) —

(a) a device or a reliable device was not available at that place or it was for any other reason impracticable to use such a device, *or*

(b) the constable who made the previous requirement had reasonable cause to believe that the device used there has not produced a reliable indication of the proportion of alcohol in the breath of the person concerned.

Since the request can be made either if a device is not available or it was impracticable to use the device or the device was defective, answers B and C are incorrect.

A requirement may be made for a sample of blood or urine, under s. 7(3) of the Act. Section 7(3)(bb) states that a requirement may be made for such a sample if a device has been used at the police station or elsewhere, but the constable who required the specimens of breath has reasonable cause to believe that the device has not produced a reliable indication of the proportion of alcohol in the breath of the person concerned. In theory, therefore, the defendant in the scenario could have been asked to provide a blood or urine sample at the station, or evidential breath samples. However, it is not mandatory to request a sample of blood or urine in these circumstances, therefore answer A is incorrect.

Road Policing, para. 3.5.5.1

Answer 5.21

Answer **A** — It was held in the case of *Pearson* v *Metropolitan Police Commissioner* [1988] RTR 276, that the requirement under s. 7 may be made of more than one person (in this instance three people were involved), in respect of the same vehicle.

Answers B and D are therefore incorrect. However, it must be believed that one of them was driving the vehicle, and answer C is incorrect.

Road Policing, para. 3.5.5.2

Answer 5.22

Answer **D** — If the machine being used at one station is unreliable, by virtue of the fact that it will not calibrate the reading correctly, it will be 'unavailable'. In this case, the driver may be taken to another station, where another machine is available, even if the driver has already provided two samples on the inaccurate machine (*Denny* v *DPP* [1990] RTR 417). Answer D is correct for this reason.

The prosecution may not use a breath test reading *and* a blood reading in the same case. If a requirement to provide blood/urine is made, that sample must be used and the prosecution may not revert to the evidence produced by the breath sample. In effect the blood sample replaces the breath sample (*Badkin* v *Chief Constable of South Yorkshire* [1988] RTR 401). Answer A is therefore incorrect.

Answer B is incorrect as two specimens of breath must be submitted as evidence to the court. It has been held that if the defendant supplies one specimen only, this will be deemed a failure to provide.

Under s. 7(3)(b) of the Road Traffic Act 1988, the defendant *may* be asked to provide a sample of blood/urine, where the device is unavailable for breath tests. However, the case of *Denny* above shows that this is not the only option available. Answer C is therefore incorrect.

Road Policing, para. 3.5.5.4

Answer 5.23

Answer **D** — All scenarios are taken from decided cases in relation to procedure under s. 7 of the Road Traffic Act 1988.

In the case of *Thompson* v *Thynne* [1986] Crim LR 629, the court held that where an officer knew at the time that the breath test machine was unavailable due to a malfunction, he or she could require a specimen of blood/urine. Answer A is correct action by the custody officer and therefore answer A is incorrect.

In the case of *Chief Constable of Kent* v *Berry* [1986] Crim LR 748, it was decided that the driver may be taken to another police station where a doctor is available. (This power extends to a registered health care professional.) Answer B is correct action by the custody officer and therefore answer B is incorrect.

In the case of *Chief Constable of Avon and Somerset* v *Kelliher* [1986] Crim LR 635, it was decided that where no trained officer was available to operate the machine, it will be 'unavailable' and a specimen of blood/urine may be requested. Answer C is correct action by the custody officer and therefore answer C is incorrect.

Where the requirement for blood/urine is made under s. 7(3)(b), that sample must be used and the prosecution cannot revert to evidence produced by the breath sample (*Badkin* v *Chief Constable of South Yorkshire* [1988] RTR 401). Answer D is incorrect action by the custody officer and therefore answer D is the correct answer to this question, which asked about incorrect action.

Road Policing, para. 3.5.5.4

Answer 5.24

Answer **C** — Where it is suspected that the driver of a vehicle, who has been requested to provide a sample under s. 7 of the Road Traffic Act 1988, is under the influence of drugs, the advice of a medical practitioner must be sought before the request is made to provide blood or urine (s. 7(3)(c)). Answers B and D are both incorrect in this respect. Answer B is also incorrect in relation to procedure, because where a person has been asked to provide a specimen of urine, there is no requirement for a medical practitioner to take the sample — it may be taken by a police officer.

When medical advice is sought in these circumstances, the doctor must give the officer a 'clear verbal' statement to the effect that the driver's condition was due to some drug, before the request is made for blood/urine (*Cole* v *DPP* [1988] RTR 224). Answer A is therefore incorrect.

Note the extended power given to registered health care professionals to take blood.

Road Policing, para. 3.5.5.5

Answer 5.25

Answer **A** — Under s. 7(7) of the Road Traffic Act 1988, when a constable is requesting the provision of a specimen under s. 7(3) a warning must be given that a failure to provide the specimen may render a person liable to prosecution. This warning is generally critical to a successful prosecution for failing to provide a specimen.

However, the warning is not needed when a driver elects to give an alternative specimen under s. 8 (i.e. choice made by the driver to replace the samples provided) — see *Hayes* v *DPP* [1993] Crim LR 966 and also *DPP* v *Jackson; Stanley* v *DPP* [1998] 3 WLR 514. Answers B and C are therefore incorrect.

Answer D is incorrect because the warning relates to *any* specimen requested under s. 7 (breath, blood or urine), even though it is not required in relation to a specimen required under s. 8.

Answer B is incorrect for a further reason — in *Bobin* v *DPP* [1999] RTR 375, it was held that as long as the information set out above is provided by a police officer, it does not matter which police officer. Therefore, the warning under s. 7(7) might be given by, for instance, the arresting officer or by the custody officer who makes the requirement for the relevant specimen.

Road Policing, paras 3.5.5.6, 3.5.5.7

Answer 5.26

Answer **C** — Section 7(4) of the Road Traffic Act 1988 states that the constable making the request can decide whether the sample to be provided should be blood or urine. However, this is subject to s. 7(4A) of the Act, which was amended to allow the sample to be taken by a registered health care professional. Under this section, where a constable decides for the purposes of subsection (4) to require the provision of a specimen of blood, the defendant will not be required to provide such a specimen if:

(a) the medical practitioner who is asked to take the specimen is of the opinion that, for medical reasons, it cannot or should not be taken; or

(b) the registered health care professional who is asked to take it is of that opinion and there is no contrary opinion from a medical practitioner.

This means that the opinion of the health care professional will be sufficient to authorise the taking of a blood sample provided that there is no contrary opinion from a doctor. Answer A is therefore incorrect.

However, this does not mean that the health care professional's opinion has to be confirmed by, or routinely referred to a doctor (this would defeat the whole purpose of the changed legislation). Answer B is therefore incorrect.

Although s. 7(4) provides the constable with the authority to make the decision as to whether the specimen should be blood or urine, this is subject to s. 7(4A) above. The statutory discretion given to the officer by s. 7(4), although wide, has to be exercised reasonably — *Joseph* v *DPP* [2003] EWHC 3078 (Admin). In *Joseph* the driver told the officer that he was a Rastafarian and therefore could not give blood. The officer's insistence that the driver give blood anyway, even though there was no reason not to take urine instead, was held to be so unreasonable as to make it unlawful. Answer D is incorrect.

Road Policing, para. 3.5.5.7

Answer 5.27

Answer **A** — Section 8(2) of the Road Traffic Act 1988 states that if the specimen of breath with the lower proportion of alcohol contains no more than 50 microgrammes of alcohol in 100 millilitres of breath, the person who provided it may claim that it should be replaced by such specimen as may be required under s. 7(4) (blood or urine) and if he or she then provides such a specimen, neither specimen of breath shall be used.

The Road Traffic Act 1988 has been amended by the Serious Organised Crime and Police Act 2005 so as to permit police to carry out an evidential breath test not only at a police station, but also at a hospital, or at or near a place (such as the roadside) where a preliminary breath test has been administered. Section 8(2A) of the 1988 Act states that if the person who makes the claim under subs. (2) above was required to provide specimens of breath under s. 7 of this Act at or near a place mentioned in subs. (2)(c) of that section (at the scene), a constable *may* arrest him or her without warrant. Since the arrest under s. 8(2A) is not mandatory, answer D is incorrect.

Answer C is incorrect because the suspect should not be given the choice as to whether he or she wishes to attend the police station once he or she has made the decision to replace the sample of breath. The power of arrest is provided to allow the constable to continue with the procedure at a police station because, naturally, a blood or urine sample may not be obtained at the scene of arrest.

Finally, once the suspect has provided two samples of breath at the scene, he or she has satisfied the requirements under s. 7 of the Act. There is no power to require the suspect to provide any further evidential samples of breath. Answer B is therefore incorrect.

Road Policing, para. 3.5.6.1

Answer 5.28

Answer **A** — When the person has provided two samples, and the lower reading is below 50 microgrammes of alcohol in 100 millilitres of breath, the person who has provided the sample may replace the breath sample with either a specimen of blood or urine (s. 8(1) and (2) of the Road Traffic Act 1988). Although the defendant is given the choice as to whether he or she wishes to replace his or her sample, the choice as to which sample will be provided will be that of the officer. Answer C is therefore incorrect.

As with s. 7 of the 1988 Act, the possibility of medical reasons for not providing blood *must* be considered. An alleged fear of needles by the driver is a relevant consideration when making this decision (*DPP* v *Jackson; Stanley* v *DPP* [1998] 3 WLR 514 and also *Johnson* v *West Yorkshire Metropolitan Police* [1986] RTR 167). Answer B is therefore incorrect.

The medical advice may be given to the officer over the telephone if appropriate (*Andrews* v *DPP* [1992] RTR 1). Answer D is therefore incorrect.

Note the extended power given to registered health care professionals to take blood.

Road Policing, para. 3.5.6.1

Answer 5.29

Answer **C** — When a fault occurs, which leads to a blood specimen being unsuitable, the prosecution may *not* use the original breath specimens to prove the person was over the limit (*Archbold* v *Jones* [1985] Crim LR 740). Answers A, B and D are therefore incorrect.

Road Policing, para. 3.5.6.1

Answer 5.30

Answer **D** — Sergeant DONELLY has not acted correctly in these circumstances. Where a driver provides one specimen only, and fails without a reasonable excuse to provide the second sample, he or she has committed the offence of 'failing to provide' a sample (*Cracknell* v *Willis* [1987] 3 All ER 801). Answers A and C are incorrect for this reason.

'Mental impairment' may provide a reasonable excuse for failing to provide a sample. However, being drunk or under stress is not in itself enough to provide a 'reasonable excuse' for failing to provide a specimen (*DPP* v *Falzarano* [2001] RTR 14). This is confirmed by the case of *DPP* v *Beech* [1992] Crim LR 64, where it was decided that where the defendant's mental capacity to understand the warning was impaired by his or her drunkenness, this was not a 'reasonable' excuse. Answer B is therefore incorrect.

Road Policing, para. 3.5.6.1

Answer 5.31

Answer **C** — The circumstances in the question mirror those in the case of *Coulter* v *DPP* [2005] EWHC 1533, where the defendant admitted to having eaten a tic-tac sweet prior to the station procedure. Initially, the magistrates' court held that there was no case to answer because the officer should have waited 20 minutes and could not show that the waiting period was not mandatory. This decision was overruled by the Divisional Court, who stated that there was nothing in s. 7 of the Road Traffic Act 1988 to indicate that the requirement to produce a specimen was unlawful if police guidelines were not followed. Answer B is incorrect.

While it is possible for a failure to follow guidelines to affect the reliability of the specimen, the court held that it was not relevant in this case as the defendant had refused to supply a specimen of breath, which is why answer C is correct, and answer D is incorrect.

The above case shows that the officer's ignorance of the guidelines would not have provided the police with protection if the defendant had provided a sample as the reliability of that sample may have been in question. Answer A is therefore incorrect.

Road Policing, para. 3.5.6.1

Answer 5.32

Answer **B** — In the case of *Wright* v *DPP* [2005] EWHC 1211, (see also *Branagan* v *DPP* [2000] RTR 235), it was held that once the defendant has elected to provide a specimen of blood, there is no reliance on the breath sample and therefore there is no requirement for the prosecution to prove that the device used to obtain the breath sample was either reliable or of an approved type. Answers A and D are therefore incorrect. The duty to show that the device was of an approved type or that it was reliable would normally fall to the prosecution, not the defence, therefore answer C is incorrect.

Road Policing, para. 3.5.6.1

Answer 5.33

Answer **B** — Under s. 15(2) of the Road Traffic Offenders Act 1988, the court must take into account any evidence of the proportion of alcohol or drugs in any specimen supplied by the accused.

However, s. 15(2) goes on to say that the court must assume that the proportion of alcohol in the accused's body at the time of the alleged offence was not less than the specimen provided (in other words at least the same). This assumption does not apply in cases where the defendant is alleged to have taken drugs. Answer B is correct for this reason.

Section 15(3) states that the accused may introduce evidence that he or she had consumed alcohol between the alleged driving offence and the provision of the specimen and that if he or she had not done so, the proportion of alcohol in his or her sample would not have exceeded the prescribed limit. Answer D is incorrect as this evidence is introduced by the defence.

However, as subs. (3) applies to the introduction of such evidence in cases involving alcohol only, it would not be applicable in the circumstances outlined. As this will not affect the ruling that the court must take evidence into account of the sample provided, answer A is incorrect.

This section applies to offences under ss. 3A, 4 or 5 of the Road Traffic Act 1988. MILLARD is accused of an offence under ss. 3A and therefore answer C is incorrect.

Road Policing, para. 3.5.8

Answer 5.34

Answer **A** — Section 15(3) of the Road Traffic Offenders Act 1988 enables a defendant to prove that alcohol had been consumed between the alleged offence and the provision of a specimen and that, if the defendant had not consumed it, then he or she would not have been over the limit or unfit to drive. In order to use the 'hip flask' defence, the defendant must show, on the balance of probabilities, that the alcohol level at the time of the offence was lower than shown in the analysis.

In *R* v *Drummond* [2002] RTR 21, it was argued that this burden on the defence contravened the presumption of innocence under Art. 6(2) of the European Convention on Human Rights. However, the Court of Appeal disagreed and held that if the defendant chose to drink after the event, it was he or she who was attempting to defeat the aim of the legislation by making a test potentially unreliable. Further, the Court held that the burden of proof should remain with the defendant on the balance of probabilities. Answers B and D are therefore incorrect.

In *DPP* v *Ellery* [2005] EWHC 2513, the magistrates' court held a different view, and accepted in trial that the defendant had drunk a can of lager after driving. The court held that once the driver proved, on the balance of probabilities that there was post-driving consumption of alcohol, the burden of proof then shifted back to the prosecution to prove, beyond reasonable doubt, that he/she was over the limit at the time of driving. This decision was overturned on appeal by the Divisional Court, where it was held that the magistrates had erred in law and that the decision in *Drummond* above should have been followed. Answer C is therefore incorrect.

Road Policing, para. 3.5.8.2

Answer 5.35

Answer **C** — Under s. 15(5) and (5A) of the Road Traffic Offenders Act 1988, the prosecution must show that the defendant, if he or she asked for one, was provided with a specimen divided and supplied as set out in the subsection. The Administrative Court has held that there is no free-standing right, either under the 1988 Act or at common law, for the defendant to be informed of his or her entitlement to a part of the sample (see *Campbell* v *DPP* [2002] EWHC 1314).

To sum up, under statute, the police do not need to inform a defendant of his or her right to be provided with a part of the specimen, and it need only be provided to the defendant when he or she has requested it. Answers A, B and D are therefore incorrect.

However, the Court in *Campbell* acknowledged that there might be occasions where the failure to tell a defendant of this entitlement might cause him or her prejudice and thereby allow the admissibility of the sample to be challenged. Therefore, although there is no specific right to be told of this entitlement, it is probably both good sense and good practice to do so.

Road Policing, para. 3.5.8.4

Answer 5.36

Answer **B** — Under s. 15(5) and (5A) of the Road Traffic Offenders Act 1988, the prosecution must show that the defendant, if he or she asked for one, was provided with a specimen divided and supplied as set out in the subsection.

Although the specimen must be divided 'at the time' it is taken and as part of the same continuing event, there is no need for it to be done in the defendant's presence (*DPP* v *Elstob* [1992] Crim LR 518). Answers A and C are incorrect.

Again, although the division of the specimen must be made at the time it is taken, there is no requirement that the defendant be provided with his or her part 'at the time' — only that it be provided within a reasonable time thereafter (see *R* v *Sharp* [1968] 2 QB 564). Answers A and D are therefore incorrect.

Road Policing, para. 3.5.8.4

Answer 5.37

Answer **D** — Section 10(1) of the Road Traffic Act 1988 states that a person required to provide a specimen of breath, blood or urine may afterwards be detained at a police station (or if the specimen was provided otherwise than at a police station, arrested and taken to and detained at a police station) if the constable has reasonable grounds for believing that, were the person to drive or attempt to drive a *mechanically propelled* vehicle on a road, he/she would commit an offence under s. 4 or s. 5 of the Act. Answer C is therefore incorrect.

Although the provision of a negative screening test would be a good indication that the person would not commit an offence under s. 4 or s. 5, there is no specific power to demand such a sample. Answer B is therefore incorrect. Similarly, there is no statutory power to retain a person's car keys to prevent them from driving (although this is common practice) and answer A is incorrect.

Road Policing, para. 3.5.9

Answer 5.38

Answer **D** — Section 10 of the Road Traffic Act 1988 allows for the detention of a person who has provided a specimen of breath, blood or urine, until it appears to a constable that were the person to drive a mechanically propelled vehicle on a road, he or she would not be committing an offence. The power does not apply if it appears to a constable that there is no likelihood of the person driving such a vehicle on a road. There is no mention of a person having been charged or reported for an offence, merely that they have been required to provide the relevant sample. Answer C is therefore incorrect.

Under s. 10(3), a constable *must* consult a medical practitioner on any question arising under this section whether a person's ability to drive properly is or might be impaired through drugs. The constable must act on such advice. This is mandatory; therefore, both answers A and B are incorrect.

Road Policing, para. 3.5.9

Answer 5.39

Answer **B** — The power under s. 7A of the Road Traffic Act 1988 allows a sample of blood to be taken from a person without his or her consent, at a hospital. It may be taken if the driver has been 'involved' in an accident and is incapable of giving consent because he or she is incapacitated due to medical reasons.

Section 7A(2)(a) states that a request under this section shall not be made to a medical practitioner 'who for the time being has any responsibility for the clinical care of the person concerned'. Note, however, that the medical practitioner in charge of the patient must still be consulted under s. 9 of the Act, as he or she will still be concerned with the physical wellbeing of the patient. This means that both doctors must be consulted — one under s. 7A and one under s. 9. Answers A and D are incorrect, as the question referred to who could take a sample under s. 7A.

Section 7A(2)(b) states that the request must be made to a police medical practitioner unless this is not reasonably practicable, in which case the request may be made to any other medical practitioner (other than the one clinically responsible for the patient). Answer C is therefore incorrect.

The Road Traffic Act has been altered to enable registered health care professionals to take a sample of blood under s. 8 of the Act (station procedure), but not to take samples at a hospital, therefore answer D is incorrect.

Road Policing, para. 3.5.10

Answer 5.40

Answer **B** — While a person is at a hospital as a patient he can be required to provide a specimen of breath for a breath test or to provide a specimen under s. 7 of the Road Traffic Act 1988 Act, provided the doctor in immediate charge of his or her case agrees. Section 7 applies to both breath samples and samples of blood/urine.

However, if a patient provides a positive reading or fails to provide a sample at a hospital, he or she cannot be arrested while still a 'patient' (s. 6(5)). Answer B is therefore correct and answer C is incorrect as, even though the officer sought permission to take the second sample, the arrest that preceded it was unlawful.

Since the arrest was unlawful, answer A is incorrect, as the patient should not have been taken to a police station in these circumstances. However, if the person had been arrested after ceasing to be a patient, she could have been taken to the station to provide a sample (see *Webber* v *DPP* [1998] RTR 111).

Answer D is incorrect as permission must be sought from a doctor for each sample that is required under s. 9(1).

Road Policing, para. 3.5.10

Answer 5.41

Answer **D** — The prohibition on sale of alcohol on moving vehicles is brought in by s. 156 of the Licensing Act 2003, which states:

(1) A person commits an offence under this section if he sells by retail alcohol on or from a vehicle at a time when the vehicle is not permanently or temporarily parked.

(2) A person guilty of an offence under this section is liable on summary conviction to imprisonment for a term not exceeding three months or to a fine not exceeding £20,000, or to both.

(3) In proceedings against a person for an offence under this section, it is a defence that —

(a) his act was due to a mistake, or to reliance on information given to him, or to an act or omission by another person, or to some other cause beyond his control, and

(b) he took all reasonable precautions and exercised all due diligence to avoid committing the offence.

The definition of vehicle for this legislation is found at s. 193 of the 2003 Act:

'vehicle' means a vehicle intended or adapted for use on roads;

Consequently answers A, B and C are incorrect.

Road Policing, para. 3.5.11.1

Answer 5.42

Answer **A** — Section 176 of the Licensing Act 2003 deals with the prohibition of alcohol sales at service areas, garages, etc.

(1) No premises licence, club premises certificate or temporary event notice has effect to authorise the sale by retail or supply of alcohol on or from excluded premises.

(2) In this section 'excluded premises' means —

(a) premises situated on land acquired or appropriated by a special road authority, and for the time being used, for the provision of facilities to be used in connection with the use of a special road provided for the use of traffic of class I (with or without other classes); or

(b) premises used primarily as a garage or which form part of premises which are primarily so used...

Looking at this definition it includes garages, and that is defined in s. 176(4)(c) as:

(c) premises are used as a garage if they are used for one or more of the following —

(i) the retailing of petrol,

(ii) the retailing of derv,

(iii) the sale of motor vehicles,
(iv) the maintenance of motor vehicles.

Any of the above will apply, and not restricted to those that sell petrol/derv, including garages on motorway service areas. Answers B, C and D are therefore incorrect.

Road Policing, para. 3.5.11.1

6 Insurance

STUDY PREPARATION

Insurance matters are straightforward and, after the detail of the previous chapter, are also relatively brief.

It is important to understand the requirements for compulsory insurance and the main related offences — including causing and permitting.

The duties on drivers and owners in relation to production of insurance documents are also important when studying this area.

QUESTIONS

Question 6.1

NEWBURY persuaded DAVIS to lend him his car to take his mother shopping. DAVIS agreed to do so, but on condition that NEWBURY arranged his own insurance. While driving DAVIS' car, NEWBURY was involved in an accident, and it was discovered that he had no insurance and that DAVIS' insurance did not cover him to drive either.

Would DAVIS be guilty of 'permitting' an offence by NEWBURY of driving without insurance?

A Yes, because permitting without insurance is an offence of absolute liability.

B No, because he told NEWBURY to insure the car before driving it, and has therefore discharged any liability for this offence.

C Yes, because even though he told NEWBURY to insure the car, he should have seen evidence that he had done so.

D No, because permitting without insurance is not an offence of absolute liability.

Question 6.2

DOUGLAS was stopped while driving GARCIA's motor vehicle on a road. He was asked to produce his driving documents, including his insurance certificate. It transpired that GARCIA's certificate of insurance had expired, and DOUGLAS did not have a policy of his own to cover his use of the vehicle. DOUGLAS claimed that he was employed by GARCIA and that he was using the vehicle in the course of employment.

If both persons were to be prosecuted, with whom does the burden of proof lie, in relation to DOUGLAS' claim to be employed by GARCIA?

A In relation to both persons, the prosecution.
B In relation to DOUGLAS, the defence; in relation to GARCIA, the prosecution.
C In relation to DOUGLAS, the prosecution; in relation to GARCIA, the defence.
D In relation to both persons, the defence.

Question 6.3

BROWN was involved in a road traffic collision while driving his employer's delivery van in the course of his work. The collision occurred about two miles from his normal delivery route. At the time, BROWN was helping a friend by giving him a lift. The insurance policy for the van allows its use in connection with business only and it is company policy not to carry passengers in vehicles. BROWN does not have an insurance policy of his own and the journey was not authorised by his company.

Would the insurance policy for the van cover BROWN's use of the vehicle at the time of the collision?

A Yes, BROWN's use of the vehicle would be covered in these circumstances.
B No, because the van was being used in a manner not authorised by BROWN'S employer.
C No, as BROWN has made a detour from his normal route, his use of the vehicle would not be covered.
D No, as the van was not being used for business purposes at the time.

Question 6.4

GRIFFITHS owned a small van, which was insured for social, domestic and pleasure purposes only. His friend, LONGMAN, was moving house and GRIFFITHS helped him by moving furniture in the van, to LONGMAN's new house. Because this entailed several trips, LONGMAN reimbursed GRIFFITHS' petrol costs.

Would GRIFFITHS be covered by his insurance policy for the use of the van in these circumstances?

A No, the use of the van would amount to a business arrangement, regardless of whether money was paid to GRIFFITHS.

B No, because money was paid to GRIFFITHS and the van was being used for purposes other than social, domestic or pleasure.

C No, either because money was paid to GRIFFITHS, or because the van was being used for purposes other than social, domestic or pleasure.

D Yes, this will not amount to a business arrangement, regardless of whether payment was paid to GRIFFITHS.

Question 6.5

SEXTON's car had broken down on the driveway and was left there for a number of months and during this time the insurance expired. SEXTON sold the car to STEPHENS and agreed to help tow it to STEPHENS' house. STEPHENS towed the car, while SEXTON sat in it and steered.

Should SEXTON's car have been insured while it was being towed?

A No, although it remained a motor vehicle, it was exempt for the purposes of insurance while it was being towed.

B Yes, it was still a motor vehicle and was not exempt from the requirement for insurance while it was being towed.

C No, it was not a motor vehicle while it was being towed; it was classed as a trailer, which is exempt from the requirement for insurance.

D Yes, it was classed as a mechanically propelled vehicle while it was being towed and was not exempt from the requirement for insurance.

Question 6.6

PAINTING works for the National Criminal Intelligence Service (NCIS). As part of her work, she is required to conduct undercover operations which involve the use of a car hired by her employers. The hire vehicle is changed every week for security purposes.

Would the vehicles be exempt from the requirement for insurance, under s. 144 of the Road Traffic Act 1988?

A Yes, as they are being used in connection with NCIS work.

B No, vehicles being used by NCIS are not covered by this exemption.

C No, only police vehicles are covered by this exemption.

D No, as the vehicles are hire vehicles.

Question 6.7

MALIK was a provisional licence holder, but was unable to afford a car and insurance. MALIK's mother owned a car and arranged for him to be a named driver on her own insurance for that vehicle. MALIK was stopped by the police one day, while driving his mother's car on the road. MALIK was accompanied by SANTOS, a full licence holder, and was complying with the terms of his provisional licence. MALIK was given an HORT/1 to produce his driving documents at a police station.

Who may produce the insurance certificate in these circumstances?

A MALIK only.

B MALIK, his mother or SANTOS only.

C MALIK or his mother only.

D Any of the above people, or any other person.

Question 6.8

Whilst on patrol in uniform, Constable BARCLAY stopped a vehicle being driven on a road by PARSONS. The officer conducted a Police National Computer (PNC) check, which revealed that PARSONS was not the registered owner, and that the vehicle was not insured. PARSONS stated that the vehicle belonged to a friend, but that she had her own certificate, which covered the use of any vehicle on a road. PARSONS, however, was unable to produce the certificate of insurance immediately, stating that it was at home.

Would Constable BARCLAY be entitled to seize the vehicle, under s. 165A(1) of the Road Traffic Act 1988, in these circumstances?

A Yes, because PARSONS was unable to produce a certificate of insurance on request by the officer.

B No, because PARSONS was not the owner of the vehicle.

C No, because PARSONS had a reasonable excuse for not producing a certificate of insurance.

D Yes, but only if the officer had reasonable grounds for believing the vehicle was uninsured.

Question 6.9

Constable BRIGHT was on mobile patrol and was attempting to stop a vehicle, which made off without stopping. The officer conducted a PNC check, which showed that the vehicle did not have insurance. Constable BRIGHT attended the address of the registered owner, HANSON, a short while later and spoke to HANSON, who admitted that the vehicle was uninsured. HANSON stated that the vehicle was parked in the detached garage in the grounds of the house.

Would Constable BRIGHT be entitled to seize the vehicle, under s. 165A(1) of the Road Traffic Act 1988, in these circumstances?

A No, because the vehicle was in a private dwelling house.

B Yes, because the vehicle was not in a private dwelling house.

C Yes, a constable may enter any premises in order to exercise this power.

D No, because the vehicle was on private property.

Question 6.10

STINTON had broken his arm and asked his friend FLEMING to drive him to the pub. On their way there, FLEMING was involved in an accident, and STINTON further damaged his broken arm. It was discovered that FLEMING was not insured to drive the vehicle. STINTON had to give up work because of the long-term damage to his arm, and made a claim for compensation to the Motor Insurers' Bureau (MIB) for damages.

Is STINTON's claim likely to succeed in these circumstances?

A No, as passengers in the offending vehicle are not entitled to claim.

B Yes, as he was not involved in a criminal act at the time of the accident.

C No, as he was a passenger who was *using* the vehicle at the time.

D Yes, as the driver of the vehicle is known and was uninsured.

Question 6.11

HOLDING was travelling as a passenger in his son's car. HOLDING's son was involved in a road traffic collision, when he collided with a stationary car. As a result, HOLDING sustained spinal injuries, which meant that he had to give up work. It was later discovered that HOLDING's son had no insurance for his car, therefore HOLDING made a claim to the Motor Insurers' Bureau (MIB), for damages as a result of the accident.

In which of the circumstances below could the MIB deny liability for the injuries caused to HOLDING?

A If it could be shown that he either knew or ought to have known that his son was not insured.

B Only if it could be shown that he actually knew that his son was not insured.

C Because HOLDING himself was not responsible for the collision, the claim cannot be refused.

D Because HOLDING's son was not involved in a criminal act, the claim cannot be refused.

ANSWERS

Answer 6.1

Answer **B** — Permitting the use of a vehicle by another without insurance is an offence under s. 143 of the Road Traffic Act 1988, and generally the offence is one of absolute liability. Answer D is therefore incorrect.

If, however, a person allows another to use his or her vehicle on the express condition that the other person insures it first, the lender cannot be guilty of 'permitting' (*Newbury* v *Davis* [1974] RTR 367). There is no mention of having to check the person's certificate before allowing him or her to drive, and presumably stating the condition will suffice. Answers A and C are therefore incorrect.

Road Policing, para. 3.6.2.1

Answer 6.2

Answer **B** — Section 143(3) of the Road Traffic Act 1988 provides a statutory defence for an employee, if he or she is using the employer's vehicle without insurance, provided he or she was not the owner of the vehicle, it was used in the course of his or her employment and he or she did not know or have any reason to believe that the vehicle was not insured. The burden of proof lies with the employee and the issue will be judged on the balance of probabilities (*R* v *Carr-Briant* [1943] All ER 156). Answers A and C are therefore incorrect.

Where an owner is suspected of committing an offence of using, causing or permitting the use of a motor vehicle on a road without insurance, the burden of proof lies with the prosecution to show the driver was acting in the course of his or her employment. The driver's statement that he or she was doing so will not in itself be sufficient to convict the owner of the offence of using (*Jones* v *DPP* [1999] RTR 1). Answers C and D are therefore incorrect.

Road Policing, paras 3.6.2, 3.6.2.2

Answer 6.3

Answer **A** — A vehicle may be insured for business purposes, and normally, if an employee deviates from the ordinary course of his or her duties, the policy will be invalidated. However, it was decided in the case of *Ballance* v *Brown* [1955] Crim LR 384 that taking a two-mile detour to give someone a lift will not necessarily invalidate the employer's insurance. Answers C and D are therefore incorrect. In a further case that emphasises this point, *Marsh* v *Moores* [1949] 2 All ER 27, it was held that an employee driving an employer's vehicle in an unauthorised manner will not negate the effect of the insurance policy. Answer B is therefore incorrect.

Road Policing, para. 3.6.2.3

Answer 6.4

Answer **D** — Lending a vehicle to a friend in return for payment reimbursing petrol costs has been held *not* to contravene s. 143 of the Road Traffic Act 1988, even when the vehicle was insured only for social, domestic and pleasure purposes (see *Lee* v *Poole* [1954] Crim LR 942). Answers B and C are incorrect for this reason. In the same case, it was held that using the vehicle to help a friend to move house will still amount to using the vehicle for social, domestic and pleasure purposes, therefore answer A is also incorrect.

Road Policing, para. 3.6.2.3

Answer 6.5

Answer **B** — When motor vehicles are being towed by other vehicles, they remain 'motor vehicles' (answers C and D are incorrect). As a result, trailers require insurance when used on roads and public places (*Milstead* v *Sexton* [1964] Crim LR 474). Answer A is incorrect.

Road Policing, para. 3.6.2.3

Answer 6.6

Answer **D** — Under s. 144 of the Road Traffic Act 1988, certain vehicles are exempt from the requirement for insurance. By virtue of s. 144(2)(ba), the exemption is extended to vehicles owned by the National Criminal Intelligence Service (NCIS) and the National Crime Squad (NCS). Answers B and C are incorrect as vehicles owned by NCIS are covered by the exemption when they are being used by the organisation by the appropriate officers and employees.

However, answer A is incorrect — the vehicles will not be exempt, as they are hire vehicles and are not owned by NCIS.

Road Policing, para. 3.6.2.5

Answer 6.7

Answer **D** — Section 165(4)(a) of the Road Traffic Act 1988 states that a person will not be convicted of an offence of failure to produce any certificate if he or she shows that —

> within seven days after the date on which the production of the certificate or other evidence was required it was produced at a police station that was specified by him at the time when its production was required,

Provided the certificate was produced the conditions under s. 165 are complied with. The certificate need not be produced in person, which means that the person who was driving the vehicle may elect *any* another person to produce it for him or her. Answers A, B and C are therefore incorrect.

Road Policing, para. 3.6.2.6

Answer 6.8

Answer **D** — Vehicles may be seized under s. 165A of the Road Traffic Act 1988, subject to certain conditions being satisfied. Under s. 165A, where a constable in uniform requests that a person produces evidence that a motor vehicle is or was not being driven in contravention of s. 143 of the Act (driving without insurance), and the person fails to produce such evidence, provided the constable has reasonable grounds for believing that the vehicle was being so driven, he or she may seize the vehicle. The power applies to any person who may produce such evidence (i.e. the driver or the owner if they are different), therefore answer B is incorrect.

Answer A is incorrect, because a vehicle may not be seized simply because a person has failed to produce a certificate of insurance. Section 165A has built-in protection for drivers in such circumstances (in line with their rights to enjoy property under the European Convention on Human Rights), because the constable must have reasonable grounds for believing that the vehicle was being driving contrary to s. 143. Imagine if this condition were not present, vehicles may be seized from any person not carrying their documents with them whilst driving!

The power under this section is based on the reasonable belief of the officer requesting the production of evidence and not based on the reasonableness of the driver's excuse for not producing a certificate of insurance. For example, a person may have a perfectly valid reason for not producing such evidence, but if the constable has reasonable grounds for believing that the vehicle is uninsured, he or she may still exercise this power. Answer C is therefore incorrect.

(Note that the powers referred to in s. 165A above also apply to circumstances where a person is believed to be driving a vehicle contrary to s. 87(1) of the Act (driving otherwise than in accordance with a licence)).

Road Policing, para. 3.6.2.7

Answer 6.9

Answer **B** — Vehicles may be seized under s. 165A of the Road Traffic Act 1988, subject to certain conditions being satisfied. Under s. 165A(4), where a constable in uniform has required a person to stop a motor vehicle and the person fails to do so, the constable may seize the vehicle where the constable has reasonable grounds for believing the vehicle is or was being driven contrary to s. 143 of the Act.

For the purposes of exercising the power under s. 165A, a constable may enter any premises other than a private dwelling house on which he or she has reasonable grounds for believing the vehicle to be. Answer C is therefore incorrect.

Under s. 165A(9)(d), the definition of a 'private dwelling house' does *not* include any garage or other structure occupied with the dwelling house or land belonging to it. Since a garage is not a private dwelling house, answer A is incorrect.

The exception above refers to private dwelling houses and not private property, therefore, if the vehicle had been parked on property which was private, but not a dwelling, it could have been seized and answer D is incorrect.

(Note that the powers referred to in s. 165A above also apply to circumstances where a person is believed to be driving a vehicle contrary to s. 87(1) of the Act (driving otherwise than in accordance with a licence)).

Road Policing, para. 3.6.2.7

Answer 6.10

Answer **C** — The purpose of the Motor Insurers' Bureau (MIB) is to provide compensation where someone is unable to pursue a valid claim against another following a road traffic accident, i.e. because the other party is not insured, not known or traceable, or insured by a company now in liquidation.

Where a person other than the driver is injured, it will be a road traffic accident. Such a person may make a claim (provided he or she does not fall within the categories listed below). Answer A is therefore incorrect.

The MIB will not compensate those who are involved in deliberate criminal acts, nor will it pursue a claim on behalf of a person who was 'using' a vehicle at a time he or she was a passenger. As the owner of the vehicle in the scenario was in it, and it was being used for his purpose, he was 'using' it without insurance and therefore cannot make a claim. Answers B and D are therefore incorrect.

Road Policing, para. 3.6.4

Answer 6.11

Answer **A** — The Motor Insurers' Bureau (MIB) will generally deny liability for any damages or loss to passengers who either knew or ought to have known that the driver was uninsured (see *Akers* v *Motor Insurance Bureau* [2003] Lloyds Rep IR 427). Answer B is incorrect, as the claim could fail if the MIB thought the passenger ought to have known that his son was uninsured. This would be the case whether or not the passenger was not responsible for the collision, therefore answer C is incorrect. Also, it is irrelevant in this particular case that the driver was not involved in a criminal act. This may be a reason for refusing a claim in some circumstances, but the claim in the scenario could be refused for the reasons listed above. Answer D is therefore incorrect.

Road Policing, para. 3.6.4

7 Safety Measures

STUDY PREPARATION

Safety measures cover a range of statutory provisions, including the requirements for seat belts, crash helmets and speed restrictions.

Once again this is a pretty straightforward area.

QUESTIONS

Question 7.1

CLEMENT was driving on a road in his car and his daughter JUDY, aged 14, was in the rear of the car and was not wearing a seat belt, even though seat belts were fitted to the vehicle. CLEMENT was wearing a seat belt himself; however, he was stopped by Constable BRIERS who saw that JUDY was not wearing hers.

Which person, if either, would commit an offence under the Road Traffic Act 1988, because of JUDY's failure to wear a seat belt?

A JUDY only, because of her age.

B Both CLEMENT and JUDY, because of JUDY's age.

C Neither person, as JUDY was in the rear of the car.

D CLEMENT only, because of JUDY's age.

Question 7.2

Section 14(4) of the Road Traffic Act 1988 allows a constable to demand the production of a medical certificate from a driver claiming exemption from having to wear a seat belt, while driving a motor vehicle on a road.

Within what time period should such a certificate be produced?

A It must be produced on request, or within 7 days at a police station.

B It must be produced on request, or within 14 days at a police station.

C The driver must have it with him or her, to be produced on request immediately.

D It must be produced on request, or within 21 days at a police station.

Question 7.3

Section 14(2)(b)(i) of the Road Traffic Act 1988 provides a general exemption in relation to the wearing of seat belts by persons in motor vehicles constructed or adapted for carrying goods while on a journey related to the transport of such goods.

Which of the following is correct, in relation to the exemption listed above?

A It applies to the driver only, for the purpose of delivering or collecting any thing.

B It applies to the driver or passenger, for the purpose of delivering or collecting any thing.

C It applies to the driver only, but only for the purpose of delivering any thing.

D It applies to the driver or passenger, but only for the purpose of delivering any thing.

Question 7.4

BRUCE drives a small van, which he uses to deliver organic vegetables. One morning, he left his place of work and delivered his product to his first customer. BRUCE was wearing his seat belt for this journey. He then drove along a main road for half a mile, to his second customer. On this occasion, he did not wear his seat belt and was stopped by a police officer on mobile patrol.

Would BRUCE be able to claim an exemption from wearing his seat belt, under s. 14(2)(b)(i) of the Road Traffic Act 1988, for the second part of his journey?

A No, because he drove further than 25 metres.

B Yes, because he drove less than 1 mile.

C No, because he drove further than 50 metres.

D Yes, because he drove less than 2 miles.

Question 7.5

ANDERSON was driving a motor vehicle on a road. There was a child sat in the rear passenger seat, aged 2. The car was old, and was not fitted with seat belts to the rear. ANDERSON was wearing a seat belt, but the child in the rear was not.

Has ANDERSON committed an offence in relation to the child's failure to wear a seat belt?

A Yes, because the child is under the age of 3.
B Yes, regardless of the age of the child.
C No, because seat belts were not fitted to the rear of the vehicle.
D Yes, because the child is under the age of 14.

Question 7.6

AMIR was driving in a family car which was fitted with air bags protecting both the driver and the front seat passenger. Accompanying AMIR in the car was a young child who was sat in a rear-facing car seat.

What regulations are in place under s. 15(1A) of the Road Traffic Act 1988, to ensure the safety of the young child in the passenger seat?

A The air bag must be de-activated, if the child is under 3 years of age.
B The child must not be placed in this seat if it is fitted with an air bag.
C The air bag must be de-activated, if the child is under 2 years of age.
D The air bag must be de-activated, regardless of the age of the child.

Question 7.7

CLARKE is an off-road motor cycle enthusiast and frequently rides his off-road motor cycle with friends in the woods near his home. He arrived one day realising that he had forgotten to take his helmet. His friend, SNOW had a spare helmet in his car and loaned it to CLARKE; however, the helmet was old and did not conform to the British Standards and was not marked to show that it was. Nevertheless, CLARKE used the helmet while riding his motor cycle.

Would SNOW be guilty of an offence under s. 17(2) of the Road Traffic Act 1988 (helmets not conforming to British Standards) by lending the helmet to CLARKE in this way?

A No, the offence is only committed when a helmet is sold to another.
B Yes, but only if CLARKE rode the motor cycle on the road.
C Yes, regardless of whether CLARKE road the motor cycle on the road.
D No, because the helmet was only loaned to CLARKE.

Question 7.8

LOUTH is on his motor cycle without wearing protective headgear.

In which of the following cases will LOUTH be exempt from the requirements of s. 16(4) of the Road Traffic Act 1988 (driving or riding on motor cycles in contravention of regulations relating to motor cycle helmets)?

A Where LOUTH is sat astride the machine, being pushed down the road by another person.

B Where LOUTH is sat astride the machine, pushing himself along using his feet.

C Where LOUTH is pushing the machine along, standing at the side of it.

D Where LOUTH is sat astride the machine being towed by a motor car.

Question 7.9

The Regulations relating to the wearing of motor cycle helmets do not apply to all motor cycles; they only apply to motor bicycles. A motor bicycle is a two-wheeled motor cycle, whether having a side-car attached thereto or not.

In counting the wheels, any two wheels in which the centre of the area in contact with the road surface is less than Z mm apart is to be treated as one wheel.

What value is Z?

A 450 mm.

B 460 mm.

C 470 mm.

D 480 mm.

Question 7.10

KRAUSER, aged 25, has a full licence to ride a motor cycle, and one day he gave his brother PAUL, aged 15, a ride on the road as a pillion passenger on the motor cycle. They were stopped by Constable FRY, because PAUL was not wearing a crash helmet. At the time, the motor cycle had a sidecar attached to it.

Who, if either, would commit an offence in these circumstances (because of PAUL's failure to wear a helmet)?

A Neither, as the motor cycle was fitted with a sidecar.

B Both, because of PAUL's age.

C KRAUSER only, because of PAUL's age.

D PAUL only, because of his age.

Question 7.11

Constable BASTABLE was conducting a speeding operation on a main road, using a hand-held speed detection camera. The officer was positioned on a long stretch of road, which led to a bend and was pointing the camera towards the bend. BETTS was travelling in a vehicle in the opposite direction, away from the officer. Upon negotiating the bend, BETTS attempted to warn other drivers approaching Constable BASTABLE by flashing the headlights of the vehicle. BETTS was seen by another police officer who was driving a police vehicle towards Constable BASTABLE.

Would BETTS' actions amount to an offence of obstructing a police constable in the execution of their duty, in these circumstances?

A Yes, merely giving such a warning can amount to an offence.

B Yes, provided it can be shown that the other drivers were exceeding the speed limit.

C No, warning drivers in such a way does not amount to an offence.

D Yes, provided it can be shown that the other drivers were exceeding the speed limit or were likely to do so.

Question 7.12

HARVEY was driving in a car at 40 mph along a road, when he was stopped by Constable UNDERWOOD. The officer believed that HARVEY was speeding, as the road was a 'restricted road'.

What physical features must be apparent for a road to be classified as a 'restricted road' under s. 82(1)(a) of the Road Traffic Regulation Act 1984?

A Street lamps less than 200 yards apart and signs signifying the 30 mph speed limit.

B Street lamps not less than 200 yards apart or signs signifying the 30 mph speed limit.

C Street lamps not more than 200 yards apart or signs signifying the 30 mph speed limit.

D Street lamps not more than 200 metres apart or signs signifying the 30 mph speed limit.

Question 7.13

GORRINGE was driving his car on a country road which was unfamiliar to him. He approached a sharp bend too quickly and lost control of his car, crashing through a hedge into a field. As a result of the collision, GORRINGE sustained severe neck injuries, which meant he had to retire from his work as a self-employed builder. GORRINGE has now instituted civil proceedings against the local authority responsible for maintaining the road, citing a failure to erect warning signs at the site of the sharp bend, to warn motorists.

Would GORRINGE be likely to succeed in his case against the local authority in these circumstances?

A Yes, the local authority has a statutory duty to promote road safety, which includes warning drivers of such danger.

B Only if it could be shown that the local authority was aware of similar incidents at the same location.

C No, the driver was responsible for his own actions.

D Yes, the local authority has a statutory duty to maintain highways, which includes warning drivers of such danger.

Question 7.14

A driver is driving at 50 mph along a road with a temporary speed restriction of 40 mph.

Which of the following statements is true in relation to 'temporary speed limits'?

A Where a driver contravenes a temporary speed restriction, corroboration is not required, but a notice of intended prosecution is.

B Where a driver contravenes a temporary speed restriction, both corroboration and a notice of intended prosecution are required.

C Where a driver contravenes a temporary speed restriction, corroboration is required, but a notice of intended prosecution is not.

D Where a driver contravenes a temporary speed restriction, neither corroboration nor a notice of intended prosecution is required.

Question 7.15

BATES works for the Serious Organised Crime Agency (SOCA) and is on a training course to learn how to drive at high speeds. BATES has been given instructions by the instructor to drive at speeds above the statutory speed limits.

Would BATES be exempt from the laws in relation to speed limits in these circumstances under the amended s. 87 of the Road Traffic Regulation Act 1984?

A Yes, provided BATES does not exceed any speed limit by more than 30 mph.
B Yes, provided BATES has been previously trained in driving at high speeds.
C Yes, the exemption applies to BATES regardless of any previous training received.
D No, the exemption does not apply to vehicles being used on training courses.

Question 7.16

Constable WOODS and Constable HUSSEIN were on duty in a marked police vehicle. They were driving along a restricted road, which had a speed limit of 30 mph. They followed DICKSON, who was driving at 40 mph in his car, for about a mile. The officers stopped DICKSON and spoke to him.

Would the officers be able to give evidence of DICKSON's speed, in order to prosecute him for the offence of speeding?

A No, their evidence does not amount to corroboration, and would not be accepted in court.
B Yes, provided it can be shown that they saw the vehicle at exactly the same time.
C Yes, the evidence that they both saw the vehicle speeding is sufficient alone to prosecute.
D Yes, corroboration is not required, as the offence took place on a restricted road.

Question 7.17

Sergeant CORNELIOUS is carrying out speed checks on the motorway using a hand-held LTI 20/20 laser speed detection device. She measures the speed of the vehicle at 109 mph and reports the driver for that offence.

In relation to the requirements for corroboration of speeding what will be the legal requirement to prove this case?

A Only the officer's evidence in relation to operating the speed detection device and the reading obtained.
B The officer's evidence together with a yearly calibration certificate of the speed detection device.
C The officer's evidence and evidence to prove the accuracy of the speed detection device after it was used.
D Only the officer's opinion that the vehicle was speeding is required.

ANSWERS

Answer 7.1

Answer **A** — It is an offence under s. 14(3) of the Road Traffic Act 1988 to drive a motor vehicle, or ride in the front or rear of a motor vehicle while not wearing an adult seat belt. Since the offences can be committed in either the front or rear of the vehicle, answer C is incorrect. The offences can only be committed by people aged 14 and over. Section 14(3) of the Act states that no person other than the person actually committing the contravention is guilty of an offence. This means that the driver of the vehicle in the scenario would commit no offence under this Act (answers B and D are therefore incorrect). Since the person in the scenario had reached the age of 14, and therefore was responsible for her own actions, she would be the only person guilty of this particular offence.

Road Policing, para. 3.7.2

Answer 7.2

Answer **A** — If a person holds a medical certificate signed by a doctor stating that the wearing of a seat belt by that person is inadvisable on medical grounds, that person will be exempt. If it is to be used in evidence in answer to a charge under s. 14(3) of the Act, the certificate must be produced to a constable on request, or within 7 days at a police station (s. 14(3)). Answers B, C and D are therefore incorrect.

Road Policing, para. 3.7.2.1

Answer 7.3

Answer **B** — Section 14(2)(b)(i) of the Road Traffic Act 1988 provides a general exemption in relation to the wearing of seat belts by persons in motor vehicles constructed or adapted for carrying goods while on a journey related to the transport of such goods. The exemption applies to both the driver and the passenger. Answers A and C are therefore incorrect. The exemption is applicable when the driver or passenger is on a journey for the purpose of delivering or collecting any thing. Answers C and D are therefore incorrect.

Road Policing, para. 3.7.2.1

Answer 7.4

Answer **C** — Section 14(2)(b)(i) of the Road Traffic Act 1988 provides a general exemption in relation to the wearing of seat belts by drivers and the passengers in motor vehicles constructed or adapted for carrying goods, while on a journey for the purpose of delivering or collecting any thing. However, reg. 6(1)(b) of the Motor Vehicles (Wearing of Seat Belts) Regulations 1993, (SI 1993/176), provides that the journey must not exceed 50 metres, (and not 25 metres, which makes answer A incorrect). Since the driver of the vehicle cannot claim an exemption in these circumstances, answers B and D are incorrect.

Road Policing, para. 3.7.2.1

Answer 7.5

Answer **A** — Under s. 15(3) of the Road Traffic Act 1988, where —

(a) a child under the age of three years is in the rear of a motor vehicle, or

(b) a child of over that age but under the age of fourteen years is in the rear of a motor vehicle and any seat belt is fitted in the rear of that vehicle,

a person must not without reasonable excuse drive the vehicle on a road unless the child is wearing a seat belt in conformity with regulations.

Therefore, because of s. 15(3)(a) above, if the child is under 3 years of age, regardless of whether seat belts are fitted to the rear of the vehicle, an offence is committed by ANDERSON. Answer C is incorrect

If the child had been over 3 years of age, but under 14, he or she would have been covered by s. 15(3)(b) above and no offence would be committed because there were no seat belts fitted to the rear of the vehicle. Answers B and D are incorrect.

Road Policing, para. 3.7.2.2

Answer 7.6

Answer **D** — Under s. 15(1A) of the Road Traffic Act 1988, where —

(a) a child is in the front of a motor vehicle other than a bus,

(b) the child is in a rear-facing child restraint device, and

(c) the passenger seat where the child is placed is protected by a front air bag,

a person must not without reasonable excuse drive the vehicle on a road unless the airbag is deactivated.

Therefore, even though there is legislation protecting the child, he or she may be placed in the front passenger seat in these circumstances, provided the air bag is deactivated (and answer B is incorrect).

There is no mention of the age of the child; therefore answers A and C are incorrect. Of course, only very young children are likely to be placed in rear-facing seats, therefore the age and size of the child will be self-regulating.

Road Policing, para. 3.7.2.2

Answer 7.7

Answer **D** — Under s. 16 of the Road Traffic Act 1988, the Secretary of State may make Regulations relating to the wearing of protective headgear by people riding motor cycles. The relevant Regulations are the Motor Cycles (Protective Helmets) Regulations 1998 (SI 1998/1807) as amended. The Regulations require every person driving or riding on a motor bicycle on a road to wear protective headgear (reg. 4). The Regulations do not apply to all motor cycles; they only apply to motor bicycles. A motor bicycle is a two wheeled motor cycle, whether having a side-car attached thereto or not.

The helmet worn must either conform to one of the British Standards specified (in reg. 5) and be marked as such or they must give a similar (or greater) degree of protection to one which meets those Standards and be of a type manufactured for motor cyclists (reg. 4(3)(a)). It is a summary offence under s. 17(2) to sell or let or hire a helmet for these purposes which does not meet the prescribed requirements. Since the offence covers more than just selling, answer A is incorrect.

That offence will be committed even if the helmet is sold for off-road use (*Losexis Ltd* v *Clarke* [1984] RTR 174), therefore answer B is incorrect. However, answer C is also incorrect, as the above offence does not apply to situations where a helmet is loaned to another, only when it is sold, let or hired.

Road Policing, para. 3.7.3

Answer 7.8

Answer **C** — Section 16 of the Road Traffic Act 1988 states:

> (4) A person who drives or rides on a motor cycle in contravention of regulations under this section is guilty of an offence...

As can be seen where the person is riding/driving the motor cycle they must wear a helmet. If you remember back to 'classifications and concepts' then you will know 'driving' takes many forms and in answers A, B and D the rider will be driving and not exempt; those answers are therefore incorrect.

The wording of reg. 4 (SI 1998/1807) suggests that no helmet is required by someone who is pushing a motor bicycle along but, if they straddled it and pedalled it along with their feet, they would require one (see *Crank* v *Brooks* [1980] RTR 441).

Road Policing, para. 3.7.3

Answer 7.9

Answer **B** — The correct answer is 460 mm, so by process of elimination answers A, C and D are incorrect.

Don't you just love questions like these?

Road Policing, para. 3.7.3

Answer 7.10

Answer **B** — Section 16(1) of the Road Traffic Act 1988 makes it an offence to ride on a motor cycle without a crash helmet. 'Ride on' includes being a pillion passenger.

If the pillion passenger is under 16, the offence is committed by both the rider and the passenger. If the pillion passenger is 16 or over, he or she is responsible alone. This is in contrast to seat belt legislation, where young passengers are not responsible for their own actions. As the person in the question was 15, both he and the driver commit the offence. Answers C and D are therefore incorrect.

A motor cycle with a sidecar attached will still be a motor bicycle for the purposes of the section and the offence is committed. Answer A is therefore incorrect. If the passenger had been sitting in the sidecar, he would have been exempt from having to wear a crash helmet (s. 16(1)).

Road Policing, para. 3.7.3.1

Answer 7.11

Answer **D** — The practice of warning other motorists of the presence of a police speed detection operation can amount to an offence of obstructing a police constable in the execution of their duty (see *DPP* v *Glendinning* [2005] EWHC 2333 and *Betts* v *Stevens* [1910] 1 KB 1). Answer C is therefore incorrect.

In such cases, it is critical that it is shown that those warned were either exceeding the speed limit or were likely to do so, (answer B is therefore incorrect). However, in the absence of such evidence, merely giving a warning to drivers who were observing the speed limit at the time will not amount to this offence, (see *Bastable* v *Little* [1907] 1 KB 59). Answer A is therefore incorrect.

Road Policing, para. 3.7.4

Answer 7.12

Answer **C** — Under s. 82(1)(a) of the Road Traffic Regulation Act 1984, a 'restricted road' is one which has a system of street lamps not more than 200 yards apart. This is the minimum requirement, and these features will mean that 30 mph signs are not required (s. 85(5)). Answer A is therefore incorrect.

The street lamps must be 200 yards apart, or less. Therefore, answers B and D are incorrect.

If a road does not have such street lamps, it must have traffic signs stating the speed limit (s. 85(4)). Conversely, a road with street lamps of less than 200 yards apart may have a higher speed limit than 30 mph, but there must be signs indicating the limit.

The speed limit for a 'restricted road' is 30 mph, and it is an offence to drive a motor vehicle on a road exceeding this limit (s. 81(1)).

It should be noted that a traffic authority can use its power to impose 'restricted' status (and therefore a speed limit of 30 mph) on a road, even though the road does not have a system of lighting as set out in s. 82(1)(a) (see *DPP* v *Evans* [2004] EWHC 2785).

Road Policing, para. 3.7.4.1

Answer 7.13

Answer **C** — Although a local authority has a general statutory duty to maintain highways and promote road safety, the failure of the local authority to erect signs does not amount to a breach of this duty (*Gorringe* v *Calderdale MBC* [2004] UKHL 15). Answers A and D are therefore incorrect. As the House of Lords put it 'drivers have to take care for themselves and drive at a safe speed irrespective of whether or not there was a warning sign; they were not entitled to suppose that the need for care on their journeys would be highlighted so as to protect them from their own negligence'. Since the driver was responsible for his own actions, answer B is also incorrect.

Road Policing, para. 3.7.4.2

Answer 7.14

Answer **D** — Section 88 of the Road Traffic Regulation Act 1984 deals with temporary speed limits. This section refers to speed restrictions and speed limits. Where a person contravenes a temporary speed restriction, corroboration is not required. A notice of intended prosecution is also not required. Answers A, B and C are therefore incorrect.

Road Policing, para. 3.7.4.3

Answer 7.15

Answer **C** — Section 87(1) of the Road Traffic Regulation Act 1984 provides that speed limits will not apply to vehicles being used for fire brigade, ambulance or police purposes, if the observance of that provision would be likely to hinder the use of the vehicle for the purpose for which it is being used on that occasion. Section 87(2) also provides an exemption to people from the Serious Organised Crime Agency. This exemption will also apply when the vehicle is being used for training persons to drive vehicles for use for Serious Organised Crime Agency purposes (see s. 87(2)(b)). Answer D is incorrect.

Under s. 87(3) of the Act, subs. (1) above does not apply unless the vehicle is being driven by a person who has satisfactorily completed a course of training in the driving of vehicles at high speed provided in accordance with regulations under this section, or is driving the vehicle as part of such a course. There is no need for BATES to have completed a previous training course, therefore answer B is incorrect.

Finally, this exemption does not refer to a maximum speed; therefore, answer A is incorrect.

Road Policing, para. 3.7.4.5

Answer 7.16

Answer **B** — Under s. 89(2) of the Road Traffic Regulation Act 1984, a person may not be convicted solely on the evidence of one person for exceeding the speed limit.

In other words, corroboration is required (unless the offence took place on a motorway). Corroboration is required when the offence takes place on a restricted road. Answer D is therefore incorrect.

Corroboration is normally provided by equipment in a police vehicle; however, two police officers may provide sufficient evidence in a case of speeding, but the court will decide how much weight to give to such evidence. It is important to show that the officers saw the vehicle at exactly the same time (*Brighty* v *Pearson* [1938] 4 All ER 127). Answers A and C are incorrect for this reason.

Road Policing, para. 3.7.4.6

Answer 7.17

Answer **D** — Remember that the question asks what is required to prove the case, not whether the person would be convicted or not.

Section 89(2) of the Road Traffic Regulation Act 1984 requires that a person prosecuted for driving a motor vehicle at a speed exceeding the limit shall not be convicted solely on the evidence of one witness to the effect that, in his or her opinion, the defendant was exceeding the speed limit. Note, however that the requirements for corroboration do not apply to general speeding offences on motorways and as such the opinion of the officer is all that is required to prove the offence; therefore answers A, B and C are incorrect.

Corroboration may be provided by the equipment in a police vehicle such as LTI 20/20 or Provida or similar speed measuring equipment (see *Nicholas* v *Penny* [1950] 2 All ER 89). Even where a device is used to measure speed, whilst it may be preferable, it is not necessary in such cases to prove the accuracy of the equipment being used (see *Darby* v *DPP* [1995] RTR 294).

Road Policing, para. 3.7.4.6

8 Other Measures Affecting Safety

STUDY PREPARATION

The areas covered by this chapter are wide and varied, ranging from the disposal of abandoned vehicles to powers under the Terrorism Act 2000.

Many of the police powers covered are particularly useful in practical situations and therefore will be of interest to those who train and test police officers.

QUESTIONS

Question 8.1

MILLS placed a handcart in a busy shopping precinct, in order to sell Christmas decorations. The stall was situated in a street, which was open to pedestrians only and where no vehicles were allowed. Constable CHADD was passing and asked MILLS to remove the handcart, as she believed it was causing an obstruction.

What, if any, obstruction is committed by MILLS?

A Obstruction of the highway.
B Obstruction of a street.
C None, as no motor vehicle is involved.
D None, as the precinct is not a 'highway' or 'street' as it is pedestrianised.

Question 8.2

TOGHILL owns a restaurant, which is managed by STEAD, who placed several tables and chairs on the wide pavement outside the restaurant to attract customers in the summer. STEAD was reported for causing an unnecessary obstruction, and when the case appeared before the magistrates was ordered to remove the obstruction. STEAD refused to do so because of the extra revenue the tables and chairs attracted.

As the owner of the restaurant, could TOGHILL be held liable for the further offence of failing to remove an obstruction, under s. 137ZA of the Highways Act 1980?

A Yes, but only if TOGHILL either consented to the continued obstruction, assisted in it or was neglectful.

B Yes, TOGHILL has absolute liability, as the owner of the restaurant.

C No, only the manager is liable for the obstruction itself and for failing to remove it.

D Yes, but only if TOGHILL either consented to the obstruction, or was neglectful.

Question 8.3

The Terrorism Act 2000 provides the police with powers to place restrictions on parking, to prevent acts of terrorism.

In relation to this power, who may authorise such restrictions, and for how long?

A A superintendent, for a period not exceeding 28 days.

B An assistant chief constable/commander, for a period not exceeding 21 days.

C An assistant chief constable/commander, for a period not exceeding 28 days.

D A chief officer of police/commander, for a period not exceeding 28 days.

Question 8.4

Constable RYAN was working in uniform as part of a team preparing for a Royal visit in a city centre. An order was in place under the Terrorism Act 2000 to regulate parking along the route the Royal cortege intended taking, to prevent acts of terrorism. Constable RYAN came across a van parked outside a shop which was situated on the route and when she found the owner, she asked him to remove the vehicle before the cortege was due to arrive in two hours. Constable RYAN returned to the location an hour later and the vehicle was still parked outside the shop.

What power, if any, does Constable RYAN have to arrest the driver of the vehicle, under s. 51(3) of the Terrorism Act 2000, in these circumstances?

A None, the driver commits no offence, as he has merely failed to remove the vehicle; he has not refused to do so.
B Arrest the driver where necessary for failing to remove the vehicle when requested.
C Arrest the driver where necessary for failing to remove the vehicle, provided he was given the proper warning.
D None, the driver may only be reported for failing to remove the vehicle when requested.

Question 8.5

PAINES lives on a main road, on a sharp bend. PAINES owns a caravan, which he keeps on his drive. He returned from holiday one evening and went to bed, forgetting to place blocks under the caravan's wheels to prevent it from moving. During the night, PAINES' caravan rolled down the drive and into the middle of the road, causing a danger to passing motorists.

Has PAINES committed an offence under s. 22A of the Road Traffic Act 1988 (causing danger to other road users)?

A No, as he did not intend to create a danger for road users.
B Yes, as he was reckless as to whether danger would be caused to road users.
C No, the offence may be committed only when a person interferes with equipment in the road.
D No, provided no injury or damage was caused by the caravan's presence.

Question 8.6

GRANT bought some fireworks, and one evening he discharged some rockets while standing on the pavement outside his house.

Has GRANT committed an offence by discharging the fireworks in these circumstances?

A No, as the fireworks were not discharged in the road.
B Yes, provided a danger was caused to people using the road.
C Yes, provided people using the road were injured, interrupted *or* endangered.
D Yes, the offence is committed by simply discharging the fireworks.

Note: This does not take account of s. 28 of the Town Police Clauses Act 1847 (wantonly discharging fireworks).

Question 8.7

AHMED used a 3.5 tonne van to deliver furniture. AHMED was delivering to a house situated in a street, which had a grass verge in the centre of the road dividing two carriageways. There were no parking spaces outside the delivery address; therefore, AHMED parked the vehicle on the grass verge until a space became available.

Has AHMED committed an offence contrary to s. 19 of the Road Traffic Act 1988, (parking commercial vehicles on verges)?

A No, because of the vehicle's weight.

B Yes, as the vehicle was parked on land in the centre of the road.

C Yes, provided the vehicle was causing a danger.

D No, as the vehicle was not parked on a verge at the side of a road.

Question 8.8

MAGUIRE owns a large flat bed trailer, which he frequently leaves outside his house, which is situated on a hill. MAGUIRE left the trailer outside the house one evening, but forgot to set the braking mechanism. As a consequence, the trailer rolled downhill, colliding with another vehicle.

Would MAGUIRE commit an offence under s. 22 of the Road Traffic Act 1988 (dangerous vehicles) in these circumstances?

A No, the trailer was not attached to a motor vehicle.

B No, this offence only applies to the condition of a vehicle.

C Yes, the offence is complete in these circumstances.

D No, this offence only applies to stationary vehicles.

Question 8.9

Local authorities are empowered to issue 'badges' under the Chronically Sick and Disabled Persons Act 1970 (as amended) for motor vehicles driven by, or used for the carriage of disabled persons.

Under what circumstances could a local authority require the return of a disabled badge from the person it was issued to?

A Where a person has misused it in a way which has led to a conviction for a relevant offence.

B Where a person has misused it in a way which has led to at least two relevant convictions.

C Where a person has misused it in a way which has led to at least three relevant convictions.
D Where a person has misused it in a way which has led to at least four relevant convictions.

Question 8.10

HARRIS was in a multi-storey car park attached to a shopping centre. The car park was operated by a private company, which owned the shopping centre, but was open to the general public at the time. The car park was covered by CCTV and the night security guard saw HARRIS climb onto the bonnet of a car and then run over the roof, jumping off the vehicle from the boot. He did this to several vehicles in the car park. The night security guard called the police and when they arrived, HARRIS was walking away from the car park.

Has HARRIS committed the offence of tampering with vehicles, under s. 25 of the Road Traffic Act 1988, in these circumstances?

A No, because the vehicles were not on a road.
B No, because the car park was not owned by the local authority.
C Yes, because the vehicles were in a public place.
D No, because he did not interfere with the brake or mechanism of the vehicles.

Question 8.11

SHAW was playing on roller blades in a leisure centre car park. The car park was owned and maintained by the local authority, but was open to the general public. The car park was built on a flat area, but the exit was on a steep hill. On several occasions, SHAW caught hold of passing vehicles, which were going down the hill. SHAW let go of the vehicles before they reached the road, but was able to accelerate to high speeds while holding onto the cars in the car park. The leisure centre manager complained to the police.

Has SHAW committed an offence under s. 26(1) of the Road Traffic Act 1988 in these circumstances?

A Yes, because SHAW was on a road or in a local authority car park.
B No, because SHAW did not get onto a vehicle.
C Yes, because SHAW was on a road or in a public place.
D No, because SHAW was not on a road.

Question 8.12

DOUGLAS lived near some woodland, which was accessible from the road. One day, he drove to the woodland in his van and abandoned a settee and two chairs in a clearing in the woods.

Has DOUGLAS committed an offence under the Refuse Disposal (Amenity) Act 1978 (disposing property on land)?

A No, the offence relates to abandoning a motor vehicle only.

B Yes, he has committed an offence in these circumstances.

C No, he has not abandoned anything on a highway or land forming part of a highway.

D No, the offence relates to abandoning a motor vehicle or part of a motor vehicle only.

Question 8.13

Section 3(1) of the Refuse Disposal (Amenity) Act 1978 imposes a duty on local authorities to remove motor vehicles that have been abandoned in their area, in certain circumstances. Before it can remove a vehicle under this section, a local authority must affix a notice to the vehicle advising the owner of its intention.

What is the period of notice that must be given by the local authority in England, to the owner of a vehicle which appears to have been abandoned and ought to be destroyed?

A 7 days.

B 28 days.

C 24 hours.

D 21 days.

Question 8.14

A cycle race was due to take place in a town centre on a Sunday. CAREY had parked a caravan on the road the night before, intending to sell burgers from it to spectators the next day. CAREY had left the caravan on double yellow lines and it was in a street which formed part of the route for the race. Constable SHEEHY was sent to the scene to arrange for its removal before the start of the race.

Did Constable SHEEHY have the authority to remove the vehicle in these circumstances?

A Yes, she had the authority to remove the vehicle herself or arrange its removal.
B No, she would have to arrange for CAREY to remove it.
C No, the vehicle was not causing an actual obstruction to people using the road.
D No, the power to remove vehicles applies to motor vehicles only.

Question 8.15

PETERS owned a trials motor cycle, which was not intended for use on roads. Near PETERS' house is an area of common land and he took his motor cycle there one day. PETERS had just started up his motor cycle and had ridden onto the land, approximately 10 yards from the road, when he was stopped by Constable MENDEZ.

Has PETERS committed an offence of driving on land other than a road, in these circumstances?

A No, as he was not driving a motor vehicle.
B Yes, as he has driven on common land other than a road.
C No, he has driven within 15 yards of the road.
D Yes, as he has driven on common land within 15 yards of the road.

Question 8.16

SHAH has hired PRICE to do some building work at his house. PRICE has hired a skip from BARRY for a period of three weeks. After a week, neighbours complain to the police that the skip is unlit during the night and is causing a danger to motorists.

Who has committed an offence in relation to the skip in these circumstances?

A SHAH only.
B PRICE only.
C PRICE and BARRY only.
D BARRY only.

Question 8.17

KAHL was approaching a zebra crossing on his motor cycle when GIBBONEY stepped on to the crossing at the last moment. KAHL did not see GIBBONEY and drove over the crossing, nearly hitting him. GIBBONEY took down the registration number of KAHL's motor cycle.

In relation to KAHL's failure to stop at the pedestrian crossing, which of the following statements is true?

A He is guilty of driving without due care and attention in these circumstances alone, which is an absolute offence.

B He is guilty of failing to stop at the crossing and driving without due care and attention.

C He is guilty of failing to stop at the crossing in these circumstances alone, which is an absolute offence.

D He is guilty of driving without due care and attention in these circumstances alone.

Question 8.18

TROTT was working as a school crossing patrol outside a school at 7.50 am. BOYCE was riding on the road on his pedal cycle, when TROTT stood in the road to allow some people to cross. As none of the people were school children, BOYCE did not stop his cycle. TROTT was wearing her uniform and exhibiting her sign at the time of the incident.

Has BOYCE committed an offence in these circumstances?

A No, because of the time of day.

B Yes, an offence has been committed.

C No, because the people crossing were not children.

D No, because he was not driving a motor vehicle.

Question 8.19

The Fire and Rescue Service have been called to a large fire at a warehouse premises. Their entrance is blocked by a motor vehicle that is locked, but has the engine running.

What action may the fire and rescue personnel do to move the vehicle?

A They may enter the vehicle if possible but may not use force to enter the vehicle unless the owner would have consented had they known the circumstances.

B They may enter the vehicle using force if necessary, but they may not drive it without the owner's consent.

C They may enter the vehicle using force if necessary and actually drive the vehicle without the owner's consent.

D They may enter the vehicle using force if necessary and actually drive the vehicle without the owner's consent and have it statutorily removed.

ANSWERS

Answer 8.1

Answer **B** — The offences of obstruction may be committed under:

- s. 137 of the Highways Act 1980, or
- reg. 103 of the Road Vehicles (Construction and Use) Regulations 1986 (SI 1986/1078), or
- s. 28 of the Town Police Clauses Act 1847 (outside London).

The offence under the Highways Act 1980 requires a person to wilfully obstruct the free passage along a highway. A 'highway' is a way over which the public has a right to pass and re-pass by foot, horse or vehicle (*Lang* v *Hindhaugh* [1986] RTR 271) and this pedestrianised area could not be a highway; Answer A is therefore incorrect.

Neither a 'street' nor a 'highway' are affected in definition by their pedestrian nature; answer D is therefore incorrect.

Also the presence of motor vehicles is not necessary for the 1980 Act or the 1986 Regulations; answer C is therefore incorrect.

Road Policing, paras 3.8.2, 3.1.3.11

Answer 8.2

Answer **A** — An offence of obstruction is committed under s. 137 of the Highways Act 1980, if a person without lawful authority or excuse, in any way wilfully obstructs the free passage along a highway. If a person convicted of this offence fails to remove an obstruction, the magistrates' court can make an order requiring them to do so. Failing to comply with such an order is a further criminal offence under s. 137ZA of the Act.

As a result of the Highways (Obstruction by Body Corporate) Act 2004, a director, manager or other officer of a company can be guilty of either of the above offences (answer C is therefore incorrect). In order for such a person to be guilty of the offence, it must be proved that the offence was committed with the consent or connivance of the officer, or that it was attributable to their neglect. Answer D is incorrect, as the offence may also be committed if the manager assisted (or connived) in causing the obstruction. Answer B is incorrect, as the offence is not one of absolute liability in respect of an officer of the company.

Road Policing, para. 3.8.2

Answer 8.3

Answer **C** — The power under the Terrorism Act 2000 is given to any officer of or above the rank of assistant chief constable/commander. Where it appears expedient to such a person to do so, he or she may authorise the imposition of prohibitions or restrictions on parking in a specified area for a period not exceeding 28 days. Answer C is therefore the only possible correct answer and answers A, B and D are incorrect.

Road Policing, para. 3.8.2.1

Answer 8.4

Answer **B** — An order may be given under s. 48 of the Terrorism Act 2000 to impose parking restrictions where it appears expedient to do so to prevent acts of terrorism, by an officer of or above the rank of assistant chief constable/commander. Any person parking in contravention of such an order commits an offence. An additional offence is committed by a person who permits a vehicle to remain at rest or fails to move such a vehicle, when ordered to do so by a constable in uniform (s. 51(3)) (refusal is not mentioned, therefore answer A is incorrect). A person will be guilty of a summary offence under s. 51(3). There is a power of arrest for all offences granted by s. 105 of the Serious Organised Crime and Police Act 2005 provided it is necessary within the strict criteria of s. 105(5) of the 2005 Act (regardless of the type of warning given); answer C is therefore incorrect. Although reporting for summons may well be available and the most appropriate method of dealing with this offence it is no longer the only method; therefore answer D is incorrect.

Road Policing, para. 3.8.2.1

Answer 8.5

Answer **A** — The offence is committed under s. 22A of the Road Traffic Act 1988, when a person intentionally and without lawful authority or reasonable excuse causes anything to be on or over the road in such circumstances that it would be obvious to a reasonable person that to do so would be dangerous.

Although PAINES could be said to have been the cause of the danger, he did not intend the act to happen. The offence is not committed when a person is merely reckless. Answer B is therefore incorrect.

Under s. 22A the offender must intend to cause anything to be in a road, *or* intend to interfere with anything. The offence may be committed if either of those situations is present. There is no need to show that the person intends to create danger. Answer C is therefore incorrect.

There is no requirement to prove that a person was injured or property was damaged; it is the potential danger that matters. Answer D is therefore incorrect.

Road Policing, para. 3.8.3

Answer 8.6

Answer **C** — Under s. 161 of the Highways Act 1980, a person commits an offence if he or she discharges any firearm or firework within 15.24 metres (50 feet) of the centre of the highway, and in consequence a user of the highway is injured, interrupted or endangered.

As the offence took place on the pavement, which would be 50 feet from the centre of the highway, answer A is incorrect.

Answer B is incorrect as a user of the highway must be injured, interrupted or endangered.

Answer D is incorrect as there must be a consequence, i.e. an injury, interruption or danger must occur as a result of the discharged firework.

Road Policing, para. 3.8.3.1

Answer 8.7

Answer **A** — Under s. 19 of the Road Traffic Act 1988, an offence is committed by a heavy commercial vehicle, which is parked wholly or in part on the verge of a road, or any land situated between two carriageways that is not a footway, or on a footway. Answer D is incorrect as the offence may be committed in the middle of the road also.

Answer B is incorrect as the vehicle was not a heavy commercial vehicle, i.e. one which exceeded 7.5 tonnes.

There is no requirement to prove that any danger was caused by the vehicle's presence. Answer C is therefore incorrect.

Road Policing, para. 3.8.4.1

Answer 8.8

Answer **A** — An offence may be committed under s. 22 of the Road Traffic Act 1988 if a person in charge of a vehicle causes or permits the vehicle or a trailer drawn by it to remain at rest on a road in such a position or in such condition or in such circumstances as to involve a danger of injury to other persons using the road, he is guilty of an offence. This suggests that although the offence applies to both motor vehicles and trailers, the trailer must be attached to the vehicle at the time of the offence (answer C is incorrect).

This offence involves presenting a danger of injury to other road users by the position, condition or circumstances of the vehicle/trailer. Answer B is therefore incorrect.

The danger presented by the condition or circumstances of the vehicle is not confined to occasions when it is stationary but will also apply to a vehicle/trailer which presents a danger by moving (such as where a driver fails to set the handbrake (*Maguire* v *Crouch* [1941] 1 KB 108)). Answer D is therefore incorrect.

Road Policing, para. 3.8.4.2

Answer 8.9

Answer **C** — A local authority may require the return of a badge and may refuse to issue such a badge if the person concerned has held and subsequently misused it in a way which has led to at least three relevant convictions (SI 2000/682 reg. 9). Since C contains the only correct answer, answers A, B and D are incorrect.

Road Policing, para. 3.8.4.4

Answer 8.10

Answer **B** — An offence is committed under s. 25 of the Road Traffic Act 1988 when a person gets onto a vehicle, or tampers with the brake or mechanism of a vehicle. Since the offence may be committed in either of these circumstances, answer D is incorrect. Offences under this section may only be committed either on a road or in a car park owned by the local authority. The offence may not be committed in any public place, therefore answer C is incorrect. Since the offence is not restricted to vehicles parked on a road, answer A is also incorrect.

Road Policing, para. 3.8.5

Answer 8.11

Answer **D** — Section 26(1) of the Road Traffic Act 1988 states:

(1) If, for the purpose of being carried, a person without lawful authority or reasonable cause takes or retains hold of, or gets on to a motor vehicle or trailer while in motion on a road he is guilty of an offence.

(2) If, for the purpose of being drawn, a person takes or retains hold of a motor vehicle or trailer while in motion on a road he is guilty of an offence.

Therefore, the offence may be committed either by a person who gets on to a vehicle or trailer while in motion, or by a person who retains hold of one. Answer B is therefore incorrect.

The offence may only take place on a road; therefore, answers A and C are incorrect. (Note that the offence of tampering or getting onto vehicles, under s. 25 of the Act, may take place on a road or parking place provided by a local authority.)

Road Policing, para. 3.8.5

Answer 8.12

Answer **B** — An offence may be committed under s. 2 of the Refuse Disposal (Amenity) Act 1978 either by abandoning a motor vehicle or anything which formed part of a motor vehicle (s. 2(1)(a)), or by abandoning any thing other than a motor vehicle (s. 2(1)(b)). Answers A and D are therefore incorrect.

The offence is complete when property, as referred to above, is abandoned either on any land forming part of the highway, or on any land in the open air. Presumably this would include private property, if it is in the open air. Answer C is therefore incorrect.

Road Policing, para. 3.8.6

Answer 8.13

Answer **C** — Section 3(1) of the Refuse Disposal (Amenity) Act 1978 states that where it appears to a local authority that a motor vehicle in their area is abandoned without lawful authority on any land in the open air or on any other land forming part of a highway, it shall be the duty of the authority, subject to the following provisions of this section, to remove the vehicle. Before it can remove a vehicle under this section, a local authority must follow the requirements of the Act and of the Removal and Disposal of Vehicles Regulations (SI 1986/183) in relation to affixing of notices advising the owner (of both the vehicle, and the land if occupied) of its intention.

In order to combat the growing problem of abandoned cars, the notice period required to be given by a local authority in relation to a vehicle which appears to have been abandoned and ought to be destroyed has been reduced from seven days to 24 hours (see reg. 10). Answers A, B and D are therefore incorrect.

It should be noted that the notice period has only been reduced to 24 hours in relation to Scotland (SSI 2002/538, reg. 3) and England (SI 2002/746, reg. 3). It still remains at seven days for Wales (as at 23 April 2005) There was a consultation exercise in 2004 on bringing Wales into line with England, but no Welsh Statutory Instrument has been produced as yet.

Note also that if the local authority has taken possession of a vehicle which is in such good condition that it ought *not* to be destroyed, the owner will have seven days in which to remove it (see reg. 14).

Road Policing, para. 3.8.6.1

Answer 8.14

Answer **A** — Under the Removal and Disposal of Vehicles Regulations 1986 (SI 1986/183), a constable may require the owner of a vehicle to remove it (reg. 3). To implement the removal of a vehicle under reg. 3, it must be broken down, causing a danger or obstruction, or committing an offence such as a parking offence.

Under reg. 4, a constable may remove a vehicle himself or herself, or arrange its removal. In these circumstances, a vehicle must have broken down, or have been abandoned without lawful authority.

In the circumstances of the question, the officer could arrange for the removal of the vehicle without contacting the owner, as the vehicle is on yellow lines without lawful authority. Answers B and C are therefore incorrect.

The 1986 Regulations are not restricted to 'motor' vehicles, and therefore a caravan will be a trailer, which in turn will be a vehicle. Answer D is therefore incorrect.

Road Policing, para. 3.8.6.2

Answer 8.15

Answer **B** — Under s. 34 of the Road Traffic Act 1988, a person commits an offence who drives a mechanically propelled vehicle on any common land, moorland or land of any other description, not being part of a road.

The offence has been reworded by the Countryside and Rights of Way Act 2000, which extended the offence to include 'mechanically propelled' vehicles, rather than 'motor vehicles'. Answer A is therefore incorrect.

As soon as the person drives on the land, he or she commits the offence. Answer D is therefore incorrect.

A defence is provided for a person who has driven onto the land within 15 yards of the road in order to park the vehicle. There is no general defence of driving within 15 yards of the road only. Answer C is therefore incorrect.

Road Policing, para. 3.8.7

Answer 8.16

Answer **D** — Under s. 139(4)(a) of the Highways Act 1980, a skip which has been deposited on a road must be 'properly lighted' during the hours of darkness. Section 139(4) states that the owner of the skip will be responsible for ensuring that it complies with the conditions imposed under the Act. Answer A is therefore incorrect.

Section 139(11) of the Act states that if a skip is either hired, or made subject of a hire purchase agreement for not less than one month, the person in possession of it will become the 'owner'. Since the builder in the scenario hired it for three weeks, which is less than a month, the actual owner, BARRY, retains responsibility for it. Answers B and C are therefore incorrect.

Road Policing, para. 3.8.8

Answer 8.17

Answer **C** — The failure by a driver to stop at a crossing in contravention of the Regulations made under the Road Traffic Regulation Act 1984 is an absolute offence. There is no need to show any particular state of mind by the driver. Further, the failure by a driver to observe the crossing Regulations will not in itself provide sufficient proof that a person has driven without due care and attention (*Gibbons* v *Kahl* [1956] 1 QB 59). Further proof would be required, although such evidence may be presented as part of a case.

Consequently, answers A, B and D are incorrect.

Road Policing, para. 3.8.9.5

Answer 8.18

Answer **B** — Section 28 of the Road Traffic Regulation Act 1984 has been amended by the Transport Act 2000. There are no longer restrictions as to the time of day that an offence may be committed (formerly the hours were 0800 hrs to 1730 hrs). Answer A is therefore incorrect.

A further effect of the 2000 Act was that school crossing patrols are no longer restricted to stopping vehicles for children to cross. They may stop vehicles to allow anyone to cross safely. Answer C is therefore incorrect.

The offence may be committed by a person who is driving or propelling a vehicle. There is no requirement for a person to be driving a motor vehicle. Answer D is therefore incorrect.

Road Policing, para. 3.8.9.6

Answer 8.19

Answer **C** — Powers in the event of emergency are given to the Fire and Rescue Service by virtue of Fire and Rescue Services Act 2004 and s. 44(2) states:

(2) In particular, an employee of a fire and rescue authority who is authorised as mentioned in subsection (1) may under that subsection —
- (a) enter premises or a place, by force if necessary, without the consent of the owner or occupier of the premises or place;
- (b) move or break into a vehicle without the consent of its owner;
- (c) close a highway;
- (d) stop and regulate traffic;
- (e) restrict the access of persons to premises or a place . . .

These wide ranging powers give fire and rescue personnel, who are authorised in writing, the practical authority to deal effectively with emergency situations. They need no consent of the owner of the property they enter (including motor vehicles); therefore answers A and B are incorrect. The power, however, does not extend to statutory removal of vehicles; answer D is therefore incorrect.

Although driving a motor vehicle without the owner's consent is an offence, this power gives the relevant personnel a defence to this and they may move it by driving it.

Road Policing, para. 3.8.10.1

9 Construction and Use

STUDY PREPARATION

The area of construction and use probably typifies what most police officers associate with road traffic legislation.

Seen by many as pedantic 'train spotter' law dealing with minor mechanical issues, construction and use legislation is in reality of some practical significance to patrol officers and the wider remit of road safety.

The level of detail that police officers and examination candidates are expected to know has been greatly reduced over recent years, but there is still quite a lot of factual information to absorb.

Although you could probably fill a book such as this with construction and use questions, you will be relieved to find that only a selection of some more relevant points has been included in this chapter.

QUESTIONS

Question 9.1

OLIVER has been issued with a defect form under the Vehicle Defect Rectification Scheme (VDRS).

In relation to this, which of the following statements is correct?

A The vehicle must be submitted for examination within 7 days and the VDRS form must be submitted to the police within 14 days.

B The vehicle must be submitted for examination and the VDRS form returned to the police within 14 days.

C The vehicle must be submitted for examination and the VDRS form returned to the police within 7 days.

D The vehicle must be submitted for examination within 14 days and the VDRS form must be submitted to the police within 21 days.

Question 9.2

Constable HEINZE attended a road traffic collision, where STONELEY's unattended car had rolled down a hill, colliding with another parked vehicle while STONELEY was in a shop. STONELEY told the officer that the handbrake had been applied to the vehicle; however, Constable HEINZE suspected that it was faulty. In order to test the handbrake, the officer pushed STONELEY's vehicle along the road with the handbrake applied for 10 metres, forming the opinion that it was, in fact, defective. Constable HEINZE was not a qualified vehicle examiner.

If STONELEY were to be prosecuted for any offences, would Constable HEINZE's evidence in relation to the handbrake be admissible in court?

A No, the vehicle must be tested either by a qualified police officer trained to examine vehicles, or a qualified Department of Transport examiner.

B No, the vehicle must be tested by a qualified police officer trained to examine vehicles.

C No, the vehicle must be tested by a qualified Department of Transport examiner.

D Yes, the vehicle may be tested by a qualified examiner, but this is not absolutely necessary.

Question 9.3

Regulation 27 of the Road Vehicles (Construction and Use) Regulations 1986 sets out the requirement for the depth of tread required for tyres fitted to motor vehicles, which are used on the road.

What is the minimum depth of tread allowed on such tyres, when the vehicle is a passenger carrying vehicle intended or adapted to carry 6 six passengers?

A 1.6 mm throughout a continuous band across the whole of the tyre, and around the entire circumference.

B 1 mm throughout a continuous band across the central three-quarters section of the tyre, and around the entire circumference.

C 1 mm throughout a continuous band across the whole of the tyre, and around the entire circumference.

D 1.6 mm throughout a continuous band across the central three-quarters section of the tyre, and around the entire circumference.

Question 9.4

Regulation 27 of the Road Vehicles (Construction and Use) Regulations 1986 sets out a number of specific defects that will make tyres unlawful. Under reg. 27(c), an offence is committed where there is a cut to the tyre.

Which of the following statements is correct, in relation to the size of the cut that must be evident, before an offence is committed?

A The tyre has a cut in excess of 25 mm or 20% of the section width of the tyre.

B The tyre has a cut in excess of 30 mm or 10% of the section width of the tyre.

C The tyre has a cut in excess of 25 mm or 10% of the section width of the tyre.

D The tyre has a cut in excess of 10 mm or 25% of the section width of the tyre.

Question 9.5

SMITHERS was reversing an agricultural tractor along a road and at the time he was towing a trailer loaded with hay. He was involved in a road traffic collision when he reversed into a vehicle which was parked at the side of the road. Constable BANNER attended the scene, and when she examined the vehicles, she noticed that two of the tyres on the trailer were devoid of tread. SMITHERS was reported for these offences; however, he pleaded not guilty in court, claiming that the trailer was exempt from the Road Vehicles (Construction and Use) Regulations 1986, in relation to tyres.

Who would bear the burden of proof, in relation to SMITHERS' claim, that the vehicle was exempt?

A The onus would be on the defence to show that the vehicle was exempt.

B The onus would be on the prosecution to show that the vehicle was not exempt.

C The question is not relevant; a trailer is not an agricultural motor vehicle and is not exempt.

D The question is not relevant; this is an absolute offence, no vehicle is exempt from the Regulations.

Question 9.6

POTTER was driving a car, while towing a trailer along the road. POTTER was stopped by Constable GILLANEY because the two rear tyres of the vehicle were so defective that the metal was in contact with the road, and sparks were flying as the vehicle was travelling along. POTTER was carrying wood in the trailer and his son was sitting on top of the load to stop it from falling off.

Ignoring any other offences that he may have committed, would POTTER be guilty of an offence under reg. 27 of the Road Vehicles (Construction and Use) Regulations 1986 (defective tyres)?

A Yes, if it could be shown there was danger to POTTER's son or that damage might have been caused to the road.

B Yes, if it could be shown there was danger to POTTER's son or that damage had been caused to the road.

C Yes, but only if it could be shown there was danger to other persons using the road, or that damage may have been caused to the road.

D No, this regulation applies only to the danger or damage caused by motor vehicles.

Question 9.7

WATSON is a taxi driver. One evening, WATSON pulled up outside a customer's house and sounded the taxi's horn several times, to attract the person's attention. The customer lived in a built up area and WATSON's taxi was stationary. The time was 11.35 pm.

Has WATSON committed an offence under reg. 99 of the Road Vehicles (Construction and Use) Regulations 1986?

A Yes, because it was after 11.00 pm and the vehicle was stationary.

B No, because it was not before 11.30 pm.

C Yes, because the vehicle was stationary.

D No, because the vehicle was stationary.

Question 9.8

WINSTON parked outside a newsagent's shop in his car. He was accompanied by BREEN, who was sitting in the front passenger seat. Before WINSTON entered the shop, he turned off the car engine, but forgot to set the handbrake. BREEN realised what had happened and pulled the handbrake up before WINSTON returned.

Has WINSTON committed the offence of 'quitting' in these circumstances?

A Yes, provided BREEN was not a full licence holder.

B No, as the engine was not left running.

C No, as BREEN was in a position to intervene.

D Yes, regardless of whether BREEN had a full licence.

Question 9.9

GRAY was driving a motor vehicle on a road, taking garden rubbish to a local tip. GRAY was towing an open trailer, which was also full of garden rubbish and GRAY's 10-year-old son, HARRY was along for the trip. There was insufficient room in the car for HARRY and GRAY sat him on the trailer, telling him to hold on to a metal bar. GRAY drove slowly to the trip, and they arrived without any incident.

Would GRAY commit an offence under s. 40A of the Road Traffic Act 1988 (dangerous use of a vehicle) in these circumstances?

A No, HARRY was sitting on a trailer; the offence applies to motor vehicles only.
B No, HARRY did not encounter any danger during the journey.
C Yes, the offence applies to motor vehicles and trailers.
D Yes, the offence applies to any vehicle.

Question 9.10

Constable QUASHIE works in a rural area and has been allocated a bicycle to assist with patrols. However, the officer is concerned that the bicycle is too slow to be used for emergency calls in the area. In order to respond quickly to such calls, Constable QUASHIE has acquired a magnetic flashing blue light, intending to fit it to the private vehicle the officer takes to and from work.

Would Constable QUASHIE be in contravention of the Road Vehicles Lighting Regulations 1989 if the blue flashing light were used on a private vehicle?

A No, if the vehicle was used for emergency purposes only.
B No, it is the purpose the vehicle is being used for that is relevant.
C No, as it will be used in the course of Constable QUASHIE's work.
D Yes, as the vehicle is not constructed or adapted for emergency work.

Question 9.11

DOMINGUEZ was driving his car on a road through a built up area at 1.00 pm, when he was stopped by Constable HIND. The officer examined DOMINGUEZ's car and discovered that the rear nearside light was defective.

What general exemption, under the Road Vehicles Lighting Regulations 1989, may DOMINGUEZ claim, to avoid prosecution for the defective light?

A None, as the exemption applies to headlamps only.
B That the defect occurred during the journey, or arrangements have been made to rectify it as soon as possible.

C That the defect occurred during the journey.

D That the defect has only recently occurred, and arrangements have been made to rectify it.

Question 9.12

The Road Vehicles (Construction and Use) (Amendment) (No. 4) Regulations 2005 allow for motor vehicles, with specific defects, to be driven to and from an MOT testing station by authorised vehicle examiners in order to ensure that the MOT tester applies the correct testing standards when conducting an MOT test.

Who may conduct such a test, and by whom must the examiner be authorised?

A A vehicle examiner from the Vehicle and Operator Services Agency, authorised by the Secretary of State.

B A vehicle examiner from the Vehicle and Operator Services Agency, authorised by their own agency.

C A vehicle examiner from the Vehicle and Operator Services Agency, authorised by the Chief of Police for the area.

D A police officer trained as a vehicle examiner, authorised by the Chief of Police for the area.

Question 9.13

SETHI took her car to JEROME's garage as the test certificate was due for renewal. When SETHI returned for her vehicle, JEROME told her that her car had passed, but repairs had been necessary to the brakes and steering. SETHI paid JEROME £200, but as she was driving home, the steering felt unsteady. She took the car to another garage, where she was told that it was unroadworthy and required further repairs.

Would JEROME have committed an offence under s. 75 of the Road Traffic Act 1988 (supplying an unroadworthy vehicle), in these circumstances?

A No, as JEROME did not sell the vehicle to SETHI.

B Yes, the offence is complete in these circumstances.

C No, as SETHI is the owner of the vehicle, JEROME could not supply it to her.

D No, because SETHI had to pay JEROME for the repairs.

Question 9.14

CRAIG realised that the test certificate on his car had expired. His friend, WALSH, owned a garage and was authorised to issue MOT certificates. CRAIG drove his car to WALSH's garage, where it failed the MOT test. CRAIG made arrangements to return the car the next day for work to be carried out, in order to pass the test.

Has CRAIG committed an offence in relation to the vehicle in these circumstances, by driving it either to or from the garage?

A Yes, on his way there only, as he had not arranged a test for the vehicle in advance.

B Yes, on his way there and on his way home, as he had not arranged to test the vehicle in advance.

C No, as he was taking the vehicle to be tested, and returning it after it had been refused a certificate.

D Yes, on his way there only; he is exempt in relation to the return journey, as the vehicle had been refused a test certificate.

Question 9.15

Constable COUZENS is an authorised vehicle examiner. Constable COUZENS was working on an initiative to examine public service vehicles (PSVs) for issues relating to road safety. With the bus company's permission, Constable COUZENS attended a local bus station and conducted tests on the brakes, steering and lights of several PSVs. During the initiative, Constable COUZENS had particular concerns about the steering of one of the older PSVs.

Did Constable COUZENS have the authority to direct this vehicle to a place to be examined, under s. 68 of the Road Traffic Act 1988?

A No, there is no power to direct stationary vehicles to a place to be examined.

B No, this only applies to vehicles on a road.

C Yes, the power may be applied in these circumstances.

D No, the power does not apply in relation to PSVs, only goods vehicles.

Question 9.16

Regulation 74 of the Road Vehicles (Construction and Use) Regulations 1986 provides a power to inspect vehicles on premises following a reportable road traffic collision.

What is the initial time period referred to in reg. 74 during which the inspection must take place, where the owner of the vehicle has not been notified of the inspection?

A Within 24 hours of the collision.
B Within 12 hours of the collision.
C Within 18 hours of the collision.
D Within 48 hours of the collision.

Question 9.17

Constable LAWRENCE was dealing with a road traffic collision involving a vehicle owned by KIM. The officer suspected that the vehicle's brakes were defective, because of comments made by KIM at the scene. KIM's vehicle was towed away from the scene by a friend and was being stored in the friend's garage. Constable LAWRENCE was an authorised vehicle examiner and attended the garage to test the brakes a few hours after the collision.

Would Constable LAWRENCE have the power to inspect the vehicle on premises, under reg. 74 of the Road Vehicles (Construction and Use) Regulations 1986?

A Yes, provided KIM consents to the examination.
B Yes, and she may enter by force if necessary.
C Yes, and she may enter by force if necessary if the garage owner is not present.
D Yes, provided the owner of the garage consents to the examination.

ANSWERS

Answer 9.1

Answer **B** — Under the Vehicle Defect Rectification Scheme (VDRS), a person issued with a defect form must submit the vehicle for examination at a Department of Transport approved testing station. The testing station will certify that the defect has been rectified and will endorse the form. There is no specific time within which this test must be conducted (and answers A and D are incorrect), however, the form itself must be submitted to the police station nominated within 14 days, (this includes time for the vehicle to be examined). Answers C and D are therefore incorrect. A copy of this form should then be forwarded to the original officer within 21 days.

Road Policing, para. 3.9.2

Answer 9.2

Answer **D** — Regulations 15–18 of the Road Vehicles (Construction and Use) Regulations 1986 (SI 1986/1078) set out the requirements as to braking systems on vehicles, together with those for their maintenance. It is not absolutely necessary for the person testing the braking system of a vehicle to be a 'qualified examiner' (see *Stoneley* v *Richardson* [1973] RTR 229. In this case, a constable testified to being able to push the defendant's car along with the handbrake applied, and the evidence was accepted by the court. Since the officer was able to conduct this test, answers A, B and C are incorrect.

Road Policing, para. 3.9.4.1

Answer 9.3

Answer **B** — Regulation 27 of the Road Vehicles (Construction and Use) Regulations 1986 (SI 1986/1078) sets out a number of specific defects that will make tyres unlawful. For passenger carrying vehicles, intended or adapted to carry fewer than 8 passengers (including) the driver), the depth of tread requirement is 1 mm. Answers A and D are incorrect. The Road Vehicles (Construction and Use) (Amendment) (No. 4) Regulations 1990 (SI 1990/1981) increased the depth of tread requirement to 1.6 mm from 1 mm for the following vehicles —

- passenger motor cars other than cars constructed or adapted to carry more than eight passengers (in addition to the driver);
- goods vehicles with a maximum gross weight not exceeding 3,500 kg;
- light trailers.

In either case, the depth of tread must be 1 mm (or 1.6 mm), throughout a continuous band across the central three-quarters section of the tyre, and around the entire circumference. Answers A and C are therefore incorrect

Road Policing, para. 3.9.4.2

Answer 9.4

Answer **C** — Regulation 27(1) of the Road Vehicles (Construction and Use) Regulations 1986 sets out a number of specific defects that will make tyres unlawful. Under reg. 27(1)(c), an offence is committed where the tyre is not maintained in such condition so that the tyre has a cut in excess of 25 mm or 10% of the section width of the tyre, whichever is the greater, measured in any direction on the outside of the tyre and deep enough to reach the ply or cord. Answers A, B and D are therefore incorrect.

Road Policing, para. 3.9.4.2

Answer 9.5

Answer **A** — Certain vehicles are exempt from the requirement to have tyres that conform to reg. 27 of the Road Vehicles (Construction and Use) Regulations 1986 (defective tyres). Answer D is incorrect, because these exemptions show that this is not an absolute offence. Amongst the vehicles which are exempt from the requirements are agricultural motor vehicles driven at not more than 20 mph and agricultural trailers being drawn at no more than 20 mph (therefore answer C is incorrect). The onus is on the defendant to show that the vehicle falls into an exempted category (answer B is incorrect).

Road Policing, para. 3.9.4.2

Answer 9.6

Answer **A** — Regulation 27 of the Road Vehicles (Construction and Use) Regulations 1986 sets out a number of specific defects that will make tyres unlawful. Under reg. 27(1)(h), an offence is committed where the tyre is not maintained in such condition as to be fit for the use to which the vehicle or trailer is being put or has a defect which might in any way cause damage to the surface of the road or damage to persons on or in the vehicle or to other persons using the road. Since this regulation does not require actual damage to have been caused, answer B is incorrect. There is no requirement to show that other road users were endangered, or if people in or on the offending vehicle may have been placed in danger, therefore answer C is incorrect. Finally, the regulation applies either to vehicles or trailers — there is no mention of 'motor vehicles', therefore answer D is incorrect.

Road Policing, para. 3.9.4.2

Answer 9.7

Answer **C** — Under reg. 99 of the Road Vehicles (Construction and Use) Regulations 1986, a person commits an offence by using the audible warning instrument while the vehicle is stationary on the road or if it is used between 11.30 pm and 7 am. The offence is complete if one of these circumstances is met. Answer B is therefore incorrect.

Answer A is incorrect as the offence is committed after 11.30 pm, not 11 pm.

Answer D is incorrect; the offence was committed because the vehicle *was* stationary.

Road Policing, para. 3.9.4.4

Answer 9.8

Answer **A** — Regulation 107 of the Road Vehicles (Construction and Use) Regulations 1986 prohibits motorists from leaving a motor vehicle unattended on a road unless the engine has been stopped *and* the handbrake has been set (*Butterworth* v *Shorthouse* [1956] Crim LR 341). This means that the offence will be committed if the driver allows either of these circumstances to occur. Answer B is therefore incorrect.

A driver will not commit an offence if the vehicle is left 'attended'. For a person to be 'attending' a vehicle in these circumstances, he or she must be licensed to drive it and be in a position to intervene. Answers C and D are incorrect; a person must be the holder of a full driving licence and be in a position to intervene.

Road Policing, para. 3.9.4.5

Answer 9.9

Answer **C** — Section 40A of the Road Traffic Act 1988 creates an offence of:

- using, causing or permitting another to use on a road,
- a motor vehicle or trailer
- which, for whatever reason, involves a danger of injury to any person.

First, the offence applies to motor vehicles and trailers only; therefore, answers A and D are incorrect.

Secondly, the offence may be committed when the use of the vehicle involves a danger of injury to any person. In *Gray* v *DPP* [1999] RTR 339, court held that a potential for injury would suffice to prove the offence. In this case, a 7-year-old boy was seen to be travelling in the open back of an uncovered jeep without any fitted restraints. The boy was steadying himself by holding on to the vehicle's roll-bars. The court held that, even though he had travelled in that way without incident many times in the past and that his father, the driver, was generally a responsible parent, the objective test as to the potential for injury meant that the offence had been committed. Answer B is therefore incorrect.

Road Policing, para. 3.9.4.11

Answer 9.10

Answer **D** — The Road Vehicles Lighting Regulations 1989 (SI 1989/1796) regulate the fitting and use of lights on vehicles. Among other things, the Regulations restrict the use of flashing blue lights used by emergency services, which are exempt from the regulations (see reg. 3).

However, emergency services personnel using their own vehicle which is not constructed or adapted for relevant 'emergency' purposes are not generally allowed to use flashing lights even if they are doing so in the course of their work (see *Ashton* v *DPP* [2005] EWHC 2729. Answers A and C are therefore incorrect.

When it comes to speed limits, the exemption for emergency service vehicles focuses on the purpose for which the vehicle was being used at that time. However, this exemption does not apply in respect of flashing blue lights, and answer B is incorrect.

Road Policing, para. 3.9.5.4

Answer 9.11

Answer **B** — It is an offence under reg. 23 of the Road Vehicles Lighting Regulations 1989 (SI 1989/1796) to use, cause or permit to be used a vehicle on a road unless the relevant lamps are clean and in good working order.

There is, however, an exemption under reg. 23(3): if the vehicle is being used during daytime hours and the defect only happened during the journey, or if arrangements have been made to rectify it with all reasonable expedition. Answers C and D are therefore incorrect.

The exemption applies to all relevant lamps, not just headlamps. Answer A is therefore incorrect.

Road Policing, para. 3.9.5.8

Answer 9.12

Answer **A** — The Road Vehicles (Construction and Use) (Amendment) (No. 4) Regulations 2005 (SI 2005/3165) and the Road Vehicles Lighting (Amendment) (No. 2) Regulations 2005 (SI 2005/3169) provide exemptions for vehicles used by Vehicle and Operator Services Agency (VOSA) examiners from having to comply with certain requirements of the Road Vehicles (Construction and Use) Regulations 1989 and the Road Vehicles Lighting Regulations 1989. The exemptions allow VOSA examiners, posing as members of the public, to drive a vehicle with specific, recorded defects, to and from an MOT testing station, in order to ensure that the MOT tester applies the correct testing standards when conducting an MOT test. Since the exemption applies to VOSA examiners, answer D is incorrect.

In order to come within the exemptions, the examiner must be authorised, in writing, by the Secretary of State. Answers B and C are therefore incorrect.

(It should be noted that an authorised person may only conduct such tests if he or she reasonably believes that the defects will not cause a danger of injury to any person while the vehicle is being so used. This means that only minor defects may be present on the vehicles, such as horns or washers not working, or rear seat belts missing, as opposed to major defects, such as those to the brakes, steering or tyres of the vehicle.)

Road Policing, para. 3.9.6

Answer 9.13

Answer **B** — It has been held that where a garage returned a vehicle to an owner, after stating that it had been repaired and had passed its MOT, when in fact it was unroadworthy, the garage committed the offence of supplying an unroadworthy vehicle (*Devon County Council* v *DB Cars* [2002] Crim LR 71). In this case, the court held that 'supplying' involved a transfer of physical control of an item from one person to another (answer D is incorrect). It is both immaterial that the owner had to pay for the repairs, and that the owner did not buy the vehicle from the offender, therefore answers A and C are incorrect.

Road Policing, para. 3.9.6

Answer 9.14

Answer **B** — There are exemptions to s. 47 of the Road Traffic Act 1988 (using a motor vehicle on a road without a test certificate), where a person is taking a vehicle to or from a testing station. However, a driver may only claim exemption if he or she is driving to or from a pre-arranged test. The key is whether the test was prearranged, and in this case it was not. Answer C is therefore incorrect.

Although they are worded differently, answers A and D are incorrect for the same reason. There is a further exemption for vehicles which have been refused test certificates. However, this exemption applies only when the vehicle is being driven, by prior arrangement, or brought from the relevant place where the work is being carried out. This exemption allows garage proprietors, who are not registered to supply test certificates, to take vehicles to and from testing stations, and again does not apply in these circumstances.

The last exemption, which again does not apply to the given facts, is where a vehicle is being towed to be broken up, following the refusal of a test certificate.

Road Policing, para. 3.9.6

Answer 9.15

Answer **B** — Section 68 of the Road Traffic Act 1988 provides a power for vehicle examiners to inspect goods vehicles, PSVs and some larger passenger carrying vehicles (answer D is incorrect). It also provides a power for a police officer in uniform to direct such a vehicle to a suitable place of inspection when found on a road, provided that that place of inspection is not more than five miles from the place where the requirement is made. Since Constable COUZENS was not examining vehicles on a road, there was no authority to direct this vehicle to a place to be examined. Answer C is incorrect.

The power conferred by s. 68 of the Road Traffic Act 1988 only applies to stationary vehicles. Therefore answer A is incorrect. (Presumably if the vehicle is moving, the officer need only stop it (using the general power under s. 163) before directing it to be driven to a place of inspection.)

Road Policing, para. 3.9.6.2

Answer 9.16

Answer **D** — Regulation 74 of the Road Vehicles (Construction and Use) Regulations 1986 provides a power to test and inspect the brakes, silencers, steering gear and tyres of any vehicle on any premises where that vehicle is located. The power applies to police officers in uniform and other authorised vehicle examiners, but may not take place unless:

- the owner of the vehicle consents;
- notice has been given to that owner (either personally or left at his/her address not less than 48 hours before the time of the proposed test/inspection, or sent to him/her by recorded delivery at least 72 hours before the proposed test/inspection); or
- the test or inspection is made within 48 hours of a reportable accident in which the vehicle was involved.

Answers A, B and C are therefore incorrect.

Road Policing, para. 3.9.6.3

Answer 9.17

Answer **A** — The power applies to police officers in uniform and other authorised vehicle examiners (see reg. 74(1)(a)–(f)). Regulation 74 provides no power of entry and stipulates that the person empowered shall produce his/her authorisation if required to do so. Answers B and C are incorrect.

Reg. 74 also provides that no such test or inspection shall be carried out unless the owner of the vehicle consents. There is no mention of the owner of the premises consenting to the examination, therefore answer D is incorrect.

Road Policing, para. 3.9.6.3

10 Driver Licensing

Please note that the questions in this chapter relate to material in the Blackstone's Police Manuals which has been excluded from the Inspectors' Exam syllabus for 2008.

STUDY PREPARATION

The law relating to driver licensing is of considerable practical significance.

You need to know how the licensing system works in terms of what licence is needed by what driver for what vehicle; you also need to know the relevant police powers in relation to licences and the attendant offences that can be committed.

Of particular importance is the offence of disqualified driving and the provisions that apply to learner drivers and their supervisors.

QUESTIONS

Question 10.1

HAY has been summonsed to appear in court for an offence under s. 87 of the Road Traffic Act 1988, of driving a motor vehicle on a road otherwise than in accordance with a licence. HAY intends pleading not guilty to the offence on two grounds: first that the vehicle had not actually been driven on a road, and secondly that the officer in the case had failed to issue her with an HORT/1 form for the production of her driving licence.

In relation to HAY's claim, which of the following statements is correct?

A It will be for HAY to prove that the vehicle was not being driven on a road, *and* that she had a licence to drive the vehicle.

B The failure of the officer in the case to issue HAY with an HORT/1 may be fatal to the case and would provide HAY with a defence to this offence.

C The prosecution need only show that HAY was driving on a road; HAY must show that she had a licence to do so.

D The prosecution must show that HAY was driving on a road *and* that she did not have a licence to do so.

Question 10.2

KLINE was driving a motor vehicle on a road, when he was stopped by Constable POPE. KLINE admitted that he was only 16 and did not possess a licence to drive the vehicle.

What power would Constable POPE have to arrest KLINE in these circumstances?

A KLINE can be arrested, where the officer believes it necessary, for driving other than in accordance with a licence.

B KLINE can be arrested, where the officer believes it necessary, for driving whilst disqualified in these circumstances.

C None at all, KLINE should be reported for summons for driving other than in accordance with a licence.

D KLINE can be arrested, where the officer believes it necessary, for driving whilst disqualified by reason of his age.

Question 10.3

All photo card licences must be renewed after a specified period of time.

What is the specified period of time allowed before renewal?

A Every 10 years.

B Every 20 years.

C On a person's 70th birthday.

D Every 5 years.

Question 10.4

BRIARS was involved in a minor road traffic collision which the police attended. BRIARS was issued with an HORT/1 form to produce a driving licence and certificate of insurance. BRIARS was due to go on holiday the next day for a week and asked a friend, HAGGER, to take the documents to the station with the HORT/1 form.

In relation to the production of both documents, which of the following statements is correct?

A HAGGER may not produce these documents; they must both be produced by BRIARS.

B HAGGER may produce the driving licence, but BRIARS must produce the certificate of insurance.

C HAGGER may produce both the driving licence and the certificate of insurance.

D HAGGER may produce the certificate of insurance, but BRIARS must produce the driving licence.

Question 10.5

Constable HERSI was on duty when she stopped BELL, a learner driver, who was driving a motor vehicle on a road. BELL was accompanied by MARTIN, who was supervising him. Constable HERSI asked BELL and MARTIN to produce their driving licences. However, only MARTIN had his with him.

From whom could Constable HERSI require a date of birth in these circumstances?

A Either, but only if she suspects BELL has committed an offence.

B Either, but only if she suspects that MARTIN is under 18.

C From BELL, as MARTIN has produced a driving licence.

D From either, but only if she suspects that MARTIN is under 21.

Question 10.6

Regulation 38 of the Motor Vehicles (Driving Licences) Regulations 1999 states that a person conducting a driving test must be satisfied as to the applicant's identity before the person is allowed to take the test.

Excluding driving tests conducted by the armed forces, which document would suffice, in order to satisfy the requirement under reg. 38 above?

A Any document with the person's photograph and signature.

B Only a passport.

C A passport or any other document with a person's photograph.

D Any document with a person's photograph, plus supporting documents with proof of the person's address.

Question 10.7

STACEY has recently left her husband KEITH and moved in with BEN. As a result, KEITH has refused to allow STACEY access to their children. She was the front seat passenger in BEN's car one day and BEN was driving, when they saw KEITH standing on the pavement waiting to cross the road. Because she was so upset by what had happened recently, STACEY persuaded BEN to drive straight at KEITH and knock him over. He did so, but fortunately KEITH sustained only minor injuries. They were both convicted of common assault at the magistrates' court, and the Crown Prosecution Service (CPS) asked the court to disqualify both defendants from driving.

Would the court be in a position to agree with the request made by the CPS in these circumstances?

A Yes, a person may be disqualified on conviction for any offence.
B Yes, but only in relation to BEN, as he was the driver.
C No, as neither has been convicted of an offence under the Road Traffic Act 1988.
D Yes, a person may be disqualified on conviction for common assault.

Question 10.8

Intelligence had been received that JANES, a disqualified driver, was driving to work regularly. Constable COOK was on patrol one morning, when he saw JANES leave his house and get into his car. Aware of the recent intelligence, Constable COOK approached the car and saw JANES place the keys in the ignition and try to start the car.

Is JANES driving whilst disqualified, under s. 103 of the Road Traffic Act 1988, in these circumstances?

A No, but JANES was attempting to drive while disqualified which is a separate offence.
B No, JANES was not driving whilst disqualified in these circumstances.
C Yes, as JANES was about to drive the vehicle and that was his clear intention.
D Yes, as by case law he is held to be driving in these circumstances.

Question 10.9

Proof is required to prove an offence of driving while disqualified under s. 103 of the Road Traffic Act 1988.

In relation to this, which of the following statements is correct?

A The prosecution will need to show the defendant was disqualified, and that he or she was aware of this fact.

B The prosecution will need to show the defendant was disqualified, but not that he or she was aware of this fact.

C The defendant will need to show that he or she was not disqualified, or that he or she was not aware of this fact.

D The offence is one of strict liability; the prosecution need only show that the defendant was driving a motor vehicle on a road.

Question 10.10

JELF was driving a motor vehicle on a road and was stopped by Constable STACEY. A Police National Computer (PNC) check revealed that JELF had recently been convicted of speeding, and had been disqualified from driving until passing a driving test. JELF was in possession of a provisional driving licence and was accompanied by FERDINAND, a fully qualified driver. The vehicle was not displaying 'L' plates.

Has JELF committed an offence in these circumstances?

A Yes, of failing to display 'L' plates.

B Yes, of driving whilst disqualified.

C Yes, of driving other than in accordance with a licence.

D No, JELF was accompanied by a fully qualified driver.

Question 10.11

BARKER has been disqualified from driving by the court until she passes her driving test. BARKER is due to attend court in relation to an offence where the prosecution allege that she failed to comply with the terms of a provisional licence holder when driving a motor vehicle on a road. BARKER intends pleading not guilty to the offence and is disputing the fact that she has failed to comply with the conditions of her licence.

Which of the following statements is correct, in relation to the burden of proof for this offence?

A The prosecution must show that BARKER was driving a motor vehicle on a road; BARKER must show she had a provisional licence and that she was driving in accordance with that licence.

B The prosecution must show that BARKER was driving a motor vehicle on a road, that she had a provisional licence and that she was not driving in accordance with that licence.

C BARKER will have to show either that she was not driving a motor vehicle on a road, or that she had a provisional licence and that she was not driving in accordance with that licence.

D The prosecution must show that BARKER was driving a motor vehicle on a road and that she had a provisional licence; BARKER must show that she was driving in accordance with that licence.

Question 10.12

STELIOS was disqualified from driving for a year and he intends applying for his licence as soon as possible after the disqualification period expires.

When will STELIOS be able to lawfully drive a motor vehicle on a road?

A As soon as he fills in the application form for a new driving licence.

B As soon as his application for a new driving licence is received by the DVLA.

C As soon as he is notified by the DVLA that his disqualification period has ended.

D As soon as he receives his new driving licence from the DVLA.

Question 10.13

When a person completes a compulsory basic training course for provisional licence holders, riding motor bicycles and mopeds, he or she is issued with a certificate.

When does such a certificate expire?

A After 1 year.

B After 2 years.

C No time limit, certificates are valid until a test is passed.

D After 3 years.

Question 10.14

An instructor taking a basic training course for learner motor bicycles and mopeds is restricted as to how many people he or she may supervise at any one time.

How many people may an instructor supervise in these circumstances?

A 4.

B 2.

C 5.

D 3.

Question 10.15

CAAN is 17 years of age and has recently passed the compulsory basic training test for a standard motor bicycle. He now holds a full licence to ride motor vehicles of that class. CAAN is desperate to buy a larger motor cycle as soon as possible, and is hoping that his full standard motor cycle licence will act as a provisional driving licence for a large motor cycle.

Would CAAN be able to use his full licence as a provisional driving licence, under s. 98(2) of the Road Traffic Act 1988, in these circumstances?

A No, because he is under 21.
B Yes, because he is over 17.
C No, because he is under 18.
D Yes, because he is over 16.

Question 10.16

MANINGA holds a full driving licence, having passed his driving test 6 months ago. MANINGA has appeared in court for driving without due care and attention. MANINGA already has 3 points on his driving licence, having been convicted for speeding as a learner driver. The court is considering issuing MANINGA with a further 4 points, which will take the penalty points on his driving licence to 7.

Could MANINGA's driving licence be revoked, under s. 3 of the Road Traffic (New Drivers) Act 1995, in these circumstances?

A Yes, provided the points MANINGA accumulated as a learner driver were accumulated in the two years before he was convicted for the second offence.
B No, MANINGA's first conviction was received as a learner driver; this legislation is aimed at new drivers only.
C Yes, provided the points MANINGA accumulated as a learner driver were accumulated in the two years before he passed his driving test.
D Yes, regardless of when MANINGA accumulated his first 3 penalty points.

Question 10.17

POTTER was supervising GREEN, who was learning to drive. As they were travelling along the road, GREEN collided with a parked car. GREEN panicked and drove off after the accident, without stopping.

Does POTTER have a responsibility for GREEN'S actions in these circumstances?

A Yes, but only if he encouraged the actions.

B No, he is only there to supervise GREEN's driving.

C No, he is only there to provide tuition for GREEN.

D Yes, he should have ensured that GREEN remained at the scene.

Question 10.18

FERDINAND was a passenger in a vehicle being driven by AZIZ, a provisional licence holder. The vehicle was fitted with L plates and FERDINAND, a full licence holder, was supervising AZIZ. The vehicle was stopped by Constable THAME, who observed that both FERDINAND and AZIZ smelled strongly of intoxicants.

In these circumstances, could a supervisor be found guilty of an offence under s. 5(1)(b) of the Road Traffic Act 1988 (in charge of a vehicle whilst over the prescribed limit)?

A No, they could only be guilty of aiding and abetting a driver who was over the prescribed limit.

B Yes, they could be in charge of the vehicle in these circumstances and be guilty of this offence.

C No, as the driver is in control of the vehicle, the supervisor could not also be in charge of it.

D Yes, but only if it could be proved that the driver was also over the prescribed limit.

Question 10.19

In order to supervise a provisional licence holder who is driving a motor vehicle on a road, the supervisor must be a 'qualified driver' under reg. 17(1) of the Motor Vehicles (Driving Licences) Regulations 1999 (SI 1999/2864).

In relation to the term 'qualified driver', which of the following statements is correct?

A They must have held a full or provisional licence for a period of three years, but the period need not necessarily be continuous.

B They must have held a full licence for a continuous period of three years.

C They must have held a full licence for a period of three years, but the period need not necessarily be continuous.

D They must have held a full or provisional licence for a continuous period of three years.

Question 10.20

ARNOLD was acting as a supervisor to MAHMOOD, who was driving a motor vehicle on a road. ARNOLD had given MAHMOOD several lessons, but was not a registered driving instructor. MAHMOOD did not pay ARNOLD directly for the lessons, but gave him money each time to cover the cost of petrol.

Does ARNOLD need to be registered to give driving lessons in these circumstances?

A No, as he was not being paid directly for the lessons.

B No, as he did not have a commercial arrangement with MAHMOOD.

C Yes, as he had a commercial arrangement with MAHMOOD.

D No, any person may charge for giving driving lessons, if they have a full licence.

Question 10.21

HEWITT is about to take a driving test and has been asked by the examiner to submit to an eyesight test prior to sitting the test. The examiner has asked HEWITT to read the registration number of a vehicle parked in the street.

How far away should the vehicle be, in order for the test to be conducted correctly?

A 20 metres.

B 20.5 metres.

C 25 metres.

D 27 metres.

Question 10.22

BELL passed her driving test a year ago. Before passing her test, BELL had accumulated points on her provisional driving licence. She has recently been issued with an endorsable fixed penalty notice and is likely to accumulate penalty points on her full driving licence.

If the combined total of points that BELL has accumulated exceeds the limit set in s. 2 of the Road Traffic (New Drivers) Act 1995, is BELL likely to have her licence revoked?

A Yes, provided the second set of points was accumulated within two years of the first set of points.

B No, the first set of points was accumulated while BELL was a provisional licence holder.

C Yes, provided the first set of points was accumulated at least two years before BELL passed her driving test.

D Yes, the Secretary of State has no alternative but to revoke BELL's driving licence in these circumstances.

Question 10.23

Sergeant BOYCOTT is called to deal with a road traffic collision on the motorway. When she arrives, she finds one of the drivers is a Pakistani national. Sergeant BOYCOTT asks the man for his driving licence and he produces a GB provisional licence. She notices he is not supervised and no 'L' plates are displayed on his vehicle. The male states he has a full Pakistani driving licence and entered the country on a permanent basis 4 months ago.

In relation to driving licence offences, which of the following is true?

A The man is driving otherwise than in accordance with a licence, as he is a provisional licence holder.

B The man is committing no offence, although he should take his GB driving test as soon as possible.

C The man is committing no offence, but must take his GB driving test within the next 8 months.

D The man is committing no offence, but must take his GB driving test within the next 12 months.

Question 10.24

AMIR was involved in a road accident during the hours of darkness. A witness stated that AMIR had caused the accident by failing to comply with a 'Give Way' sign. AMIR admitted to Constable WARE that he normally wore contact lenses, but had forgotten to wear them that night.

Under what conditions may Constable WARE require AMIR to submit to an eyesight test?

A In daylight conditions, while wearing his contact lenses.

B In darkness, without his contact lenses.

C In darkness, while wearing his contact lenses.

D In daylight conditions, without his contact lenses.

ANSWERS

Answer 10.1

Answer **C** — In proving the offence under s. 87 of the Road Traffic Act 1988, it is for the *prosecution* to show that the defendant was driving on a road. Answer A is therefore incorrect.

It is for the defendant to show that he or she had a licence to drive that class of vehicle (*John* v *Humphries* [1955] 1 All ER 793). In spite of this, it would be prudent for the prosecution to gather such evidence as is available to them, such as DVLA records. This was confirmed in *DPP* v *Hay* [2006] RTR 3, where the court held that once the prosecution had proved the defendant had driven on a public highway, it is for him or her to show that he or she had a driving licence and insurance as those matters were within the defendant's knowledge. Answer D is therefore incorrect.

It was also held in *Hay* above that there is no obligation for the police to serve a request for production of the relevant driving documents (e.g. by issuing an HORT/1 form). Answer B is therefore incorrect.

Road Policing, para. 3.10.2

Answer 10.2

Answer **A** — Even though a person who drives a certain class of vehicle under age will be 'disqualified' from holding a licence, that person will not commit an offence of disqualified driving under s. 103 of the Road Traffic Act 1988. They will commit an offence of driving other than accordance with a licence, under s. 87(1) of the Act. Answers B, and D are all incorrect for this reason.

As all offences are now potentially arrestable it is wrong to say that there is no power of arrest at all; answer C is therefore incorrect. The officer can arrest, but would have to show it was necessary within the strict criteria laid down in the Serious Organised Crime and Police Act 2005, s. 105(5).

Road Policing, para. 3.10.2

Answer 10.3

Answer **A** — The licence is renewable every 10 years, presumably because unfortunately, as we get older, our appearance changes! Answers B, C and D are therefore incorrect.

Road Policing, para. 3.10.3.1

Answer 10.4

Answer **D** — Driving licences must be produced in person, whereas a certificate of insurance may be produced by any person. Since answer D is the only one containing the correct combination, answers A, B and C are incorrect.

Road Policing, para. 3.10.4.1

Answer 10.5

Answer **D** — The power to demand a person's date of birth in these circumstances is given by s. 164(2) of the Road Traffic Act 1988. If a person is driving a vehicle, and fails to produce a driving licence as requested, the officer may ask for his or her date of birth. There is no requirement to suspect that an offence has been committed. Answer A is therefore incorrect.

A constable may also demand a date of birth from a person who is supervising a driver, if he or she suspects that person to be under 21 years of age. Answer B is therefore incorrect. This power would also apply even if the person has produced a driving licence, provided the constable had reason to suspect that he or she is under 21. Answer C is therefore incorrect.

Road Policing, para. 3.10.4.2

Answer 10.6

Answer **B** — The only document that is acceptable as proof of identity in respect of a driving test will be a passport (except in relation to tests run by the armed forces). Answers A, C and D are therefore incorrect.

Road Policing, para. 3.10.7

Answer 10.7

Answer **D** — The Powers of Criminal Courts (Sentencing) Act 2000 gives courts the power to disqualify any defendant from holding or obtaining a driving licence when convicting that person of any criminal offence. Similarly, where a court convicts a person of common assault or of any assault, or of aiding and abetting, counselling or procuring or inciting such an assault, the court may disqualify that person when the offence was committed by the use of a vehicle. Therefore, although STACEY was not actually driving the vehicle, she could still be disqualified by the court because of the joint nature of the offence and answer B is incorrect. Answer A is incorrect, as this power does not apply to *any* offence. Similarly, answer C is incorrect as the power may be applied even when the person has not been convicted of an offence under the Road Traffic Act 1988.

Road Policing, para. 3.10.8

Answer 10.8

Answer **B** — Under s. 103 of the Road Traffic Act 1988, a person is guilty of an offence if, while disqualified for holding or obtaining a licence, he drives a motor vehicle on a road. The person must be driving to commit the offence, therefore answer C is incorrect.

The offence of driving while disqualified is triable summarily. This means that there is no offence of attempting to commit the offence, and answer A is incorrect. The person in the question was not driving, as he was engaged in a preparatory act. Therefore he will not be guilty of an offence in these circumstances (which is why answer D is incorrect).

Recent case law has extended the meaning of 'driving' to include occasions where a person has been driving but has temporarily ceased (see *Shackleton* v *Chief Constable of Lancashire Police* [2001] EWCA Civ 1975, when a police officer saw a disqualified driver 'jogging' away from a car). Further guidance can be found in the case of *Pinner* v *Everett* [1969] 1 WLR 1266, when the House of Lords found that each case should be taken on its merits, but that a person could be driving if he or she:

- had actually stopped driving or intended carrying on (e.g. at a set of traffic lights);
- was still driving;
- had arrived at his or her destination or intended to continue to a further location;
- had been prevented or dissuaded from driving by someone else.

None of the above fit the circumstances in the question, as the person was about to start a fresh journey.

Road Policing, para. 3.10.8

Answer 10.9

Answer **B** — The offence under s. 103 of the Road Traffic Act 1988 is one of strict liability. However, the prosecution will need to show more than just the fact that the defendant was driving a motor vehicle on a road. Answer D is therefore incorrect.

The prosecution will need to prove that the defendant was, in fact, a disqualified driver. As the onus is on the prosecution, answer C is incorrect.

However, there is no need for the prosecution to prove that the defendant knew of the disqualification (*Taylor* v *Kenyon* [1952] 2 All ER 726). Answer A is therefore incorrect.

Road Policing, para. 3.10.8

Answer 10.10

Answer **B** — Where a person has been disqualified by the court until a test is passed, he or she has to comply with the requirements of a provisional licence holder. This will include driving with 'L' plates and being accompanied by a qualified passenger. Answer D is therefore incorrect.

If a person fails to comply with these requirements, he or she commits the offence of disqualified driving under s. 103 of the Road Traffic Act 1988 (*Scott* v *Jelf* [1974] RTR 256). Answers A and C are therefore incorrect.

Road Policing, para. 3.10.8.1

Answer 10.11

Answer **A** — A person disqualified from holding a licence until he or she has passed another driving test is a disqualified person for the purposes of s. 103 of the Road Traffic Act 1988. That person may only drive a motor vehicle on a road if he or she obtains a provisional driving licence and drives in accordance with the terms of that licence (i.e. being accompanied by a qualified passenger and using 'L' plates).

It will fall to the driver to show that, not only did he or she have a provisional driving licence at the time, but that he or she was driving in accordance with the conditions of that licence (see *DPP* v *Barker* [2004] EWHC 2502). Answers B and D are therefore incorrect. The burden is on the prosecution to show that a defendant was the driver of the vehicle at a particular time; it is not down to the defendant to prove the opposite, therefore answer C is incorrect.

Road Policing, para. 3.10.8.1

Answer 10.12

Answer **B** — Once a period of disqualification ends, the person may apply for another licence. On application for another licence the person falls within the category of someone who 'has held and is entitled to obtain' a licence under s. 88 of the Road Traffic Act 1988. Section 88 provides an exemption to the offence of driving otherwise than in accordance with a licence (s. 87).

The person can begin to drive again as soon as a proper application has been received by the Driver and Vehicle Licensing Agency. There is no need for the person to wait to receive the driving licence (answer D is incorrect). The person will not be notified by the DVLA that the disqualification period has expired — the onus is with the driver to apply and answer C is incorrect. Lastly, answer A is incorrect because the application must be received by the DVLA, not merely filled out by the applicant.

It should be noted that if a person drives before applying for a new licence he or she commits the offence under s. 87 (driving otherwise than in accordance with a licence).

Road Policing, para. 3.10.8.2

Answer 10.13

Answer **B** — When a person completes a compulsory basic training course, he or she is issued with a certificate which is valid for two years, therefore answers A, C and D are incorrect.

Road Policing, para. 3.10.9.1

Answer 10.14

Answer **D** — An instructor taking a training course for motor cycles and mopeds (compulsory basic training) may not supervise more than three provisional licence holders at one time. This is in contrast to an instructor taking a training course for 'large motor cycles' (direct access course). Here, the number of students an instructor can safely train is two. Answers A, B and C are therefore incorrect.

Road Policing, para. 3.10.9.1

Answer 10.15

Answer **A** — Section 98(2) of the Road Traffic Act 1988 provides that a person holding a full licence for certain classes of vehicle may drive motor vehicles of other classes as if authorised by a provisional licence for those other classes.

However, under reg. 19(5) of the Motor Vehicles (Driving Licences) Regulations 1999 (SI 1999/2864) a person who holds a licence for a learner or standard motor bicycle but who is under the age of 21 cannot use that licence as a provisional licence for a large motor bicycle. Answer C is incorrect, because even if a person has reached the age of 18, the driving licence could not be used in this way until he or she has reached the age of 21. For the same reason, it is irrelevant whether the person is over 16 or 17 — he or she would still be ineligible to ride large motor cycles in any circumstances. Answers B and D are therefore incorrect.

Road Policing, para. 3.10.9.2

Answer 10.16

Answer **D** — Section 3 of the Road Traffic (New Drivers) Act 1995 sets out a probationary period of two years beginning when the driver passed a test of competence. If, during that time, the driver receives six or more penalty points on his or her licence, the full entitlement to drive will be lost and the driver will have to pass another test of competence in the category of vehicle which he or she was entitled to drive (s. 4).

The Divisional Court has confirmed that, if a driver attracts penalty points as a result of an offence committed while he or she held a provisional licence and then receives further points in the first two years of holding a full licence taking him or her to six or more points in all, the Secretary of State has no alternative but to revoke the licence under the provisions of s. 3 (see *R (On the Application of Adebowale)* v *Bradford Crown Court* [2004] EWHC 1741). Answer B is incorrect as the accumulation of points as a learner driver will count towards the six or more penalty points for s. 3.

The two-year probationary period commences when the person passes his/her test. There is no mention in s. 3 (or the *Adebowale* case above) of a time limit in respect of accumulating the penalty points as a learner driver. It can be assumed, therefore, that these points will count regardless of when they were accumulated. Answers A and C are therefore incorrect.

Road Policing, para. 3.10.11

Answer 10.17

Answer **D** — A person supervising a learner driver is required not to provide tuition for the learner, but to 'supervise'. That means doing whatever might reasonably be expected to prevent the learner driver from acting carelessly or endangering others (see *Rubie* v *Faulkner* [1940] 1 All ER 285). Answer C is therefore incorrect.

Supervising requires some positive action on behalf of the supervisor, and these duties extend to ensuring compliance with other legislative requirements, such as remaining at the scene of an accident (*Bentley* v *Mullen* [1986] RTR 7), or remaining sober when doing so (*DPP* v *Janman* [2004] EWHC 101). Answer B is therefore incorrect. There is no need to show encouragement to commit the offence, merely that the supervisor did not act to prevent the actions. Answer A is therefore incorrect.

Road Policing, para. 3.10.9.5

Answer 10.18

Answer **B** — The situation of a passenger being drunk whilst supervising a learner driver was considered by the Divisional Court in *DPP* v *Janman* [2004] EWHC 101. There it was held that, in any ordinary case, the person supervising a learner driver was in control of the vehicle and this was the obvious and normal consequence of their role. Therefore, if the supervisor's blood/alcohol level exceeded the prescribed limit, he or she would commit the offence under s. 5(1)(b) of the Road Traffic Act 1988 simply by supervising a learner driver on a road or in a public place.

Additionally, the contingent role of the supervisor, whereby he or she has to be ready to take actual control of the vehicle at any point, means that it is almost impossible for him/her to argue the defence under s. 5(2) of the Act — because that defence requires the defendant to show that there was no likelihood of his/her driving while still over the limit. The whole purpose of supervising a learner is to intervene as and when it becomes necessary and therefore there is every likelihood of the supervisor having to drive during the journey. Answer C is therefore incorrect.

A 'supervisor' can also be convicted of aiding and abetting where the learner driver is over the prescribed limit or unfit through drink or drugs (*Crampton* v *Fish* [1970] Crim LR 235). This is a separate issue from the *Janman* case above, which shows that a supervisor could commit *either* offence, depending on the circumstances, and one is not dependant upon the other. Answers A and D are therefore incorrect.

Road Policing, paras 3.10.9.5, 3.5.3

Answer 10.19

Answer **C** — Under reg. 17(1) of the Motor Vehicles (Driving Licences) Regulations 1999, a person is a 'qualified driver' for the purpose of the regs. if he or she is 21 years of age or over, holds a relevant licence and has the relevant driving experience (there are further provisions in the regs. relating to supervising disabled drivers).

A 'relevant licence' means a full licence (including a Northern Ireland or Community licence) authorising the driving of vehicles of the same class as the vehicle being driven by the provisional licence holder (reg. 17(3)(c)). Answers A and D are incorrect, as this will not include a provisional licence. 'Relevant driving experience' is defined at reg. 17(3)(d). Generally a person will have relevant driving experience if they have held the relevant full licence for a continuous *or* aggregate period of not less than three years. Since there may be a break in the three-year period, answers B and D are incorrect.

Road Policing, para. 3.10.9.5

Answer 10.20

Answer **C** — Any person may give driving lessons provided they do not charge money or money's worth in return. If a person wants to give driving lessons for payment, he or she must be registered in accordance with the provisions of Part V of the Road Traffic Act 1988. Answers A and D are therefore incorrect.

In the case of *Mahmood* v *Vehicle Inspectorate* (1998) 18 WRTLB 1, it was held by the Divisional Court that what mattered was that the instructor had some sort of arrangement with the learner driver and that the arrangement had a 'commercial flavour'. The fact that Arnold was receiving money's worth (a payment for petrol) may amount to a 'commercial flavour' for the purposes of this legislation. Answer B is therefore incorrect.

Road Policing, para. 3.10.10

Answer 10.21

Answer **D** — Generally, where a police officer requires a person to submit to an eyesight test because the driver is suspected of having driven with uncorrected defective eyesight (under s. 96(1) of the Road Traffic Act 1988), the required distance for reading a registration number is 20.5 metres.

However, there is a greater requirement imposed on applicants taking driving tests. In these cases, the relevant distance is 27 metres (see the Motor Cars (Driving Instruction) Regulations 2005 (SI 2005/1902) (as amended)). Answers A, B and C are therefore incorrect.

Road Policing, para. 3.10.13.1

Answer 10.22

Answer **D** — The Road Traffic (New Drivers) Act 1995 sets out a probationary period of two years, during which a person may have his or her driving licence revoked by the Secretary of State after accumulating six or more penalty points. In *R (on the application of Adebowale)* v *Bradford Crown Court* [2004] EWHC 1741, the Divisional Court held that if a driver attracts penalty points on a provisional driving licence, and then receives further points in the first two years of holding a full licence, taking him or her to six or more points in all, the Secretary of State has no alternative but to revoke the licence under the provisions of s. 3 of the Act. Answer B is therefore incorrect.

The Divisional Court's ruling does not state that the points on the full driving licence have to be accumulated within two years of any other points, (therefore answer A is incorrect). Additionally, the ruling does not state that the points on the provisional driving licence have to be accumulated at least two years before a person passes their driving test. Answer C is therefore incorrect.

Road Policing, para. 3.10.11

Answer 10.23

Answer **C** — The entitlement of drivers living outside the United Kingdom to drive here under the authority of their overseas permits is governed by the Motor Vehicles (International Circulation) Order 1975 (SI 1975/1208).

If such drivers hold a domestic or Convention driving permit issued abroad or a British Forces driving licence, they may drive the vehicles covered by those authorities in Great Britain for one year (Art. 2).

Regulation 80 of the Motor Vehicles (Driving Licences) Regulations 1999 (SI 1999/2864) makes similar provisions in relation to people who become resident in the United Kingdom.

That permit allows the holder to take a driving test in that 12-month period. If they do not do so successfully then they will need a GB provisional licence.

Visitors and new residents holding a valid driving licence may also use that licence during the first 12 months and, if they apply for a GB provisional licence during that period, they will be exempt from the conditions imposed on provisional licence holders (reg. 18).

Logically the answer is clear. If the person wishes to sit a driving test they require a provisional licence. The possession of this does not suddenly lose their entitlement to drive on their own driving permit for a period of 12 months. The male from Pakistan is not committing a driving licence offence; answer A is therefore incorrect. The male must take his driving test within the 12-month period from entering the country; having been here for 4 months that leaves 8 to pass the test; answers B and D are therefore incorrect.

Road Policing, para. 3.10.12

Answer 10.24

Answer **D** — Under s. 96(2) of the Road Traffic Act 1988, where a constable has reason to suspect that a person may be guilty of driving a motor vehicle on a road with defective eyesight, he or she may require the driver to submit to an eyesight test, which would include the ability to read a registration mark fixed to a motor vehicle from 20.5 metres (or if the registration mark is a new type with narrower characters, 20 metres) (refusing to do so is an offence under s. 96(3)).

The specific requirements as to eyesight are set out at regs. 72–73 and Sch. 8 to the Motor Vehicles (Driving Licences) Regulations 1999 (SI 1999/2864). The driver must be given the eyesight test in good light, whilst wearing corrective lenses, if they were worn when the person drove the motor vehicle on a road. This means that if the person was not wearing corrective lenses, they must take the test without them. Answers A and C are therefore incorrect. Even if the offence took place in darkness, the driver must take the test in good light. Answers B and C are incorrect for this reason.

Road Policing, para. 3.10.13.1

11 Fixed Penalty System

Please note that the questions in this chapter relate to material in the Blackstone's Police Manuals which has been excluded from the Inspectors' Exam syllabus for 2008.

> **STUDY PREPARATION**
>
> The fixed penalty notice (FPN) system is pretty straightforward. Understand the principles behind it and you will realise that the system is simply designed to speed up the administration of some common offences which won't result in disqualification.
>
> The flowcharts in the *Blackstone's Road Traffic Manual* are useful in seeing the whole system at work.

QUESTIONS

Question 11.1

Constable KERR stopped GROGAN, who was driving a motor vehicle on a road. Upon examining the vehicle, Constable KERR noticed that the tread on one of the front tyres fitted to the vehicle was below the legal limit. Constable KERR intended issuing GROGAN with an endorsable fixed penalty notice, but GROGAN stated that the vehicle belonged to his brother and that he was using it with his permission. He claimed that his brother was responsible for maintaining the vehicle.

Could Constable KERR issue a fixed penalty notice to GROGAN's brother for permitting the use of the vehicle, in these circumstances?

A Yes, a notice could be given to the driver for using and to the owner for permitting.

B No, a fixed penalty notice may only be issued to the driver of a vehicle.

C No, a fixed penalty notice may not be issued to a person who is guilty of permitting an offence.

D No, the officer would only have been able to do so if it could be proved that his brother *caused* GROGAN to drive the vehicle.

Question 11.2

RICHIE was stopped by Constable WELLER for a speeding offence. Constable WELLER intended issuing RICHIE with a fixed penalty notice for the offence. RICHIE did not have his driving licence with him, but stated that there were some points on it, although he could not remember how many.

Under what circumstances could RICHIE be made to surrender his driving licence for the offence, if he produces it within 7 days?

A None, as he did not have it with him at the time, he should be reported for the offence.

B He must produce it to a constable or authorised person, provided he is not likely to exceed 11 points for this offence.

C He must produce it to a constable in uniform, provided he is not likely to exceed 12 points for this offence.

D He must produce it to a constable or authorised person, provided he is not likely to exceed 12 points for this offence.

Question 11.3

Where a person has failed to pay a fixed penalty notice during the enforcement period, the police are entitled to ask the court for an increase in the amount payable for the notice.

What increase are the police allowed to ask for in these circumstances?

A Equal to twice the amount of the original notice.

B Equal to 1.5 times the amount of the original notice.

C Equal to 3 times the amount of the original notice.

D Equal to 5 times the amount of the original notice.

Question 11.4

SAGGERS was sent a letter by the Clerk to the Justices in his area that a vehicle registered to him had been issued with a fixed penalty notice, and that the notice had not been paid. The letter stated that the police intended asking the court to increase the sum payable on the fixed penalty notice. SAGGERS had sold the vehicle recently to a neighbour, but had forgotten to notify the DVLA. His intention was to return the notice to the Clerk, declaring that he was not the person given the fixed penalty notice.

What period of time is allowed for SAGGERS to return such a declaration to the court?

A Within 21 days from the time the notice was sent by the Clerk.
B Within 14 days of receiving the notice from the Clerk.
C Within 14 days from the time the notice was sent from the Clerk.
D Within 21 days of receiving the notice from the Clerk.

Question 11.5

Under the Functions of Traffic Wardens (Amendment) Order 1986, traffic wardens are given certain powers to issue fixed penalty notices.

What kind of fixed penalty notices may a traffic warden issue?

A Both non-endorsable and endorsable, for any offence.
B Non-endorsable only, for certain offences only.
C Both non-endorsable and endorsable, but only for certain offences.
D Non-endorsable for all offences; endorsable for certain offences only.

Question 11.6

Section 75(8)(1)(a) of the Road Traffic Offenders Act 1988 specifies a period during which a person issued with a conditional offer of a fixed penalty may make a payment in order to avoid attending court.

What is the length of the specified period?

A 14 days.
B 21 days.
C 1 month.
D 28 days.

Question 11.7

SANCHEZ was driving on a road with a 30 mph speed limit, when she activated a speed camera at 45 mph. SANCHEZ was sent a conditional offer of a fixed penalty notice, which she duly returned, together with her driving licence and payment for the offence. The administrating office noticed that SANCHEZ already had points on her driving licence and, taking into account the new offence, she would now be liable for disqualification.

What should the administrating office now do with SANCHEZ's driving licence and payment for the offence?

A Forward the payment to the court and the driving licence to the police.
B Forward both the payment and the driving licence to the court.
C Return the payment to SANCHEZ and forward the driving licence to the court.
D Return both the payment and the driving licence to SANCHEZ and notify the police.

ANSWERS

Answer 11.1

Answer **C** — Section 51(2) of the Road Traffic Offenders Act 1988 specifies that a person may be issued only with a fixed penalty notice if the offence relates to the 'use' of the vehicle on a road. The system does not apply to those who 'cause' or 'permit' the use of a vehicle on a road while an offence is being committed. Answers A and D are therefore incorrect.

Fixed penalty notices may be issued to a person not driving a vehicle — most non-endorsable notices are issued to stationary vehicles, and even though an endorsable notice may not be fixed to a stationary vehicle, there is nothing to prevent one being issued to the owner of a vehicle which is, for example, parked outside a house and committing an offence. Answer B is therefore incorrect.

Road Policing, para. 3.11.3

Answer 11.2

Answer **B** — A person may be issued with a fixed penalty notice (FPN) if he or she commits an offence to which the procedure applies (in this case, an endorsable offence). The person may not be issued with a FPN if he or she would be liable for disqualification if convicted for the offence. A person would be disqualified under the 'totting up' procedure if his or her driving licence shows 12 points or more. Answer D is incorrect as a FPN may be issued only if the points are likely to exceed 11 points, not 12.

If a person does not have his or her licence at the time of the offence, he or she may be required to produce it within seven days and therefore answer A is incorrect. There is a safeguard built in here, because if it is discovered at this stage that the penalty points are likely to reach 12 points, the driving licence will not be surrendered.

Lastly, the driving licence may be produced either to a constable in uniform *or* to an authorised person, such as an enquiry clerk at a police station. Answer C is therefore incorrect.

Road Policing, para. 3.11.4.1

Answer 11.3

Answer **B** — If the person has not paid a fixed penalty, or given notice requesting a court hearing by the end of the enforcement period, the police can register a sum equal to 1.5 times the amount of the penalty for enforcement against that person (s. 55(3) of the Road Traffic Offenders Act 1988). Answers A, C and D are therefore incorrect.

Road Policing, para. 3.11.4.1

Answer 11.4

Answer **D** — If a person receives a notice stating that a fixed penalty notice (FPN) has not been paid, he or she may serve a statutory declaration to the court to the effect either that he or she was not the person who was given the FPN, or that he or she has given a notice requesting a court hearing. In either case, the statutory notice must be made and served within 21 days of receiving the notice from the clerk (and not 21 days from the time the notice was sent). Answers A, B and C are therefore incorrect.

Road Policing, para. 3.11.4.1

Answer 11.5

Answer **C** — Under the Functions of Traffic Wardens (Amendment) Order 1986 (SI 1986/1328) a traffic warden has the same powers as a constable to issue fixed penalty notices (FPNs), for both endorsable and non-endorsable offences. Answer B is incorrect. Traffic wardens may issue FPNs of both types, for certain offences only, therefore, answers A and D are incorrect.

Road Policing, para. 3.11.4.2

Answer 11.6

Answer **D** — Under s. 75(8)(a) of the Road Traffic Offenders Act 1988, the specified period is 28 days and therefore answers A, B and C are incorrect.

Road Policing, para. 3.11.5

Answer 11.7

Answer **D** — Under s. 76(4) of the Road Traffic Offenders Act 1988, where a person is sent a conditional offer of a fixed penalty notice (FPN), and that person is liable for disqualification, the payment and the licence will be returned to the defendant and the police will be notified. This would give the police the opportunity to proceed by way of summons. Consequently, answers A, B and C are incorrect.

Road Policing, para. 3.11.5

12 Forgery and Falsification of Documents

Please note that the questions in this chapter relate to material in the Blackstone's Police Manuals which has been excluded from the Inspectors Exam syllabus for 2008.

STUDY PREPARATION

The end of the road — or at least road traffic.

There are relatively few offences involving forgery and falsification, though as much road traffic law — and its enforcement — relies upon records, these offences are more relevant than they may at first appear.

QUESTIONS

Question 12.1

UNION was stopped while driving PIPER's car on a road and was asked to produce his driving documents. UNION did not have his own policy of insurance. PIPER did not have insurance either, as he had failed to keep up his monthly payments and his insurance company had cancelled the policy. PIPER was still in possession of the insurance certificate, and he lent this to UNION for him to produce it. UNION was aware of the situation when he produced the documents.

Have either UNION or PIPER committed the offence of forgery of documents under s. 173 of the Road Traffic Act 1988?

A Yes, UNION only commits this offence in these circumstances.

B Yes, UNION and PIPER both commit this offence in these circumstances.

C Yes, PIPER only commits this offence in these circumstances.

D Yes, UNION commits this offence; PIPER is guilty of aiding and abetting.

Question 12.2

STANGER runs an international road haulage company and has recently married. He wishes to start another business in his wife's name and applies for an international road haulage permit for her. His wife has a recent conviction for drink driving, although she is currently not disqualified. STANGER is unaware of this, as his wife does not wish him to know, and claims on the application form that neither he nor his wife have any previous convictions. As a result a permit is issued, when it may not have been had the conviction been declared.

Has an offence of making a false statement to obtain the grant of an international road haulage permit been committed?

A Yes, as a false statement has been made, his wife knows it to be false and it is an application on her behalf.

B Yes, as he has gained an advantage by not declaring the conviction in that a permit was issued that may not have been.

C No, because he had no intention of deceiving the issuers of the permit when he made the decleration.

D No, because he did not knowingly make a false statement as he was unaware of the conviction.

Question 12.3

Section 174 of the Road Traffic Act 1988 deals with the offence of making false statements and withholding information.

What would the prosecution need to show, in order to prove an offence under this section?

A The offence is one of specific intent, and the prosecution must show that the defendant gained from the transaction.

B There is no need for the prosecution to prove intent, or that the defendant gained from the transaction.

C The offence is one of specific intent, but there is no need to show the defendant gained from the transaction.

D There is no need to prove intent, but the prosecution must show the defendant gained from the transaction.

Question 12.4

Whilst on mobile patrol, Constable FRENCH stopped a large goods vehicle being driven by PARSONS. Constable FRENCH was not an authorised vehicle examiner, but had recently been studying to go on a traffic officer's course and decided to examine the vehicle. The officer noticed that the plate attached to the vehicle authorising its 'plated' weight had been interfered with in that the characters and words had been scratched out. Constable FRENCH suspected that the plate had been fraudulently altered.

What powers would Constable FRENCH have in respect of the vehicle and the plate attached to it, under s. 176 of the Road Traffic Act 1988?

A Constable FRENCH may seize the vehicle to which the plate is attached until it has been examined.

B None, Constable FRENCH will have to call an authorised vehicle examiner, who may detach the plate from the vehicle.

C Constable FRENCH may detach the plate, and cause it to be examined by an authorised vehicle examiner.

D None, the power under this section relates to seizing documents and a plate is not a document.

ANSWERS

Answer 12.1

Answer **B** — Under s. 173(1)(b) of the Road Traffic Act 1988, a person commits an offence if, with intent to deceive, he or she lends to, or allows to be used by any other person, a document or other thing to which the section applies. Certificates of insurance are covered, and where a person produced a certificate of insurance issued under a policy which had expired, the offence is made out (*R* v *Cleghorn* [1938] 3 All ER 398). Therefore, PIPER is guilty of the full offence, by lending/allowing UNION to use the insurance certificate.

Under s. 173(1)(a) of the Road Traffic Act 1988 a person is guilty of an offence if, with intent to deceive, he or she 'uses' a document to which this section applies. UNION is guilty of 'using' the document when he produces it. Answers A, C and D are therefore incorrect.

Road Policing, para. 3.12.2.1

Answer 12.2

Answer **D** — There is a specific offence under s. 174(1)(e) of the Road Traffic Act 1988, of knowingly making a false statement for the purpose of obtaining the grant of an international road haulage permit.

However such an offence must be committed knowingly whether the application is for himself or another person. Knowingly is very different from intent, and this offence requires no intent; answer C is therefore incorrect. Without the 'knowingly' the offence is not complete even though his wife knew about the conviction (although this may negate the legality of the actual permit); answers A and B are therefore incorrect.

Road Policing, para. 3.12.2.2

Answer 12.3

Answer **C** — The offence under s. 174 of the Road Traffic Act 1988 is one of specific intent; therefore answers B and D are incorrect.

There is no need to show that the person actually gained anything, or brought about the desired consequences (see *Jones* v *Meatyard* [1939] 1 All ER 140). Answers A and D are incorrect for this reason.

Road Policing, para. 3.12.2.2

Answer 12.4

Answer **B** — Section 176(4) of the Road Traffic Act 1988 provides a power to seize either a document or a plate from a vehicle where the constable reasonably believes that an offence under s. 173 (forgery or falsification) has occurred. Since the power applies to plates on a vehicle also, answer D is incorrect. However, the officer removing the plate must be an examiner appointed under s. 66A of the Act. Since Constable FRENCH is not an authorised vehicle examiner, one must be called to the scene to detach the plate and answer C is incorrect. The power under this section relates to seizing documents (or plates) and does not allow the seizure of a vehicle by the officer. Answer A is therefore incorrect.

Road Policing, para. 3.12.2.4

Question Checklist

The checklist below is designed to help you keep track of your progress when answering the multiple-choice questions. If you fill this in after one attempt at each question, you will be able to check how many you have got right and which questions you need to revisit a second time. Also available on-line, to download visit: www.blackstonespolicemanuals.com.

	First attempt Correct (✓)	Second attempt Correct (✓)
1 Classifications and Concepts		
1.1		
1.2		
1.3		
1.4		
1.5		
1.6		
1.7		
1.8		
1.9		
1.10		
1.11		
1.12		
1.13		
1.14		
1.15		
1.16		
1.17		
1.18		
1.19		
1.20		
1.21		
1.22		
1.23		
1.24		
1.25		
1.26		
1.27		
2 Offences Involving Standards of Driving		
2.1		
2.2		
2.3		
2.4		
2.5		
2.6		
2.7		
2.8		
2.9		
2.10		
2.11		
2.12		
2.13		
2.14		
2.15		

	First attempt Correct (✓)	Second attempt Correct (✓)
2.16		
2.17		
2.18		
2.19		
2.20		
2.21		
2.22		
2.23		
2.24		
2.25		
3 Notices of Intended Prosecution		
3.1		
3.2		
3.3		
3.4		
3.5		
3.6		
3.7		
3.8		
3.9		
4 Accidents and Collisions		
4.1		
4.2		
4.3		
4.4		
4.5		
4.6		
4.7		
4.8		
4.9		
4.10		
4.11		
4.12		
4.13		
5 Drink, Drugs and Driving		
5.1		
5.2		

	First attempt Correct (✓)	Second attempt Correct (✓)
5.3		
5.4		
5.5		
5.6		
5.7		
5.8		
5.9		
5.10		
5.11		
5.12		
5.13		
5.14		
5.15		
5.16		
5.17		
5.18		
5.19		
5.20		
5.21		
5.22		
5.23		
5.24		
5.25		
5.26		
5.27		
5.28		
5.29		
5.30		
5.31		
5.32		
5.33		
5.34		
5.35		
5.36		
5.37		
5.38		
5.39		
5.40		
5.41		
5.42		

	First attempt Correct (✓)	Second attempt Correct (✓)
6 Insurance		
6.1		
6.2		
6.3		
6.4		
6.5		
6.6		
6.7		
6.8		
6.9		
6.10		
6.11		
7 Safety Measures		
7.1		
7.2		
7.3		
7.4		
7.5		
7.6		
7.7		
7.8		
7.9		
7.10		
7.11		
7.12		
7.13		
7.14		
7.15		
7.16		
7.17		
8 Other Measures Affecting Safety		
8.1		
8.2		
8.3		
8.4		
8.5		

	First attempt Correct (✓)	Second attempt Correct (✓)
8.6		
8.7		
8.8		
8.9		
8.10		
8.11		
8.12		
8.13		
8.14		
8.15		
8.16		
8.17		
8.18		
8.19		
9 Construction and Use		
9.1		
9.2		
9.3		
9.4		
9.5		
9.6		
9.7		
9.8		
9.9		
9.10		
9.11		
9.12		
9.13		
9.14		
9.15		
9.16		
9.17		
10 Driver Licensing		
10.1		
10.2		
10.3		
10.4		
10.5		

	First attempt Correct (✓)	Second attempt Correct (✓)
10.6		
10.7		
10.8		
10.9		
10.10		
10.11		
10.12		
10.13		
10.14		
10.15		
10.16		
10.17		
10.18		
10.19		
10.20		
10.21		
10.22		

	First attempt Correct (✓)	Second attempt Correct (✓)
10.23		
10.24		
11 Fixed Penalty System		
11.1		
11.2		
11.3		
11.4		
11.5		
11.6		
11.7		
12 Forgery and Falsification of Documents		
12.1		
12.2		
12.3		
12.4		

ESSENTIAL—EFFECTIVE—PRACTICAL

*Indispensable **ONLINE** study-aids for all police officers sitting the Part I promotion examinations*

Fully updated for the 2008 syllabus

Blackstone's Police Manuals 2008 Online

FULLY UPDATED for the 2008 syllabus as of 21 September 2007

- Fast, desktop access to the complete text of all four Blackstone's Police Manuals
- Find the information you need quickly and easily by using the powerful search engine via the table of contents or the consolidated A–Z index
- Extensive cross-referencing ensures you can easily revise all relevant subject areas together

Subscriptions: **£78.00** (12 months) | **£58.00** (8 months)

Blackstone's Police Q&As 2008 Online*

- An online Multiple Choice Questions database—the essential study-aid for all police officers sitting the Part 1 promotion examinations
- Over 1500 questions—all of the same format and difficulty as the actual exam
- Choose the number of questions from a single subject or a mixture of all four
- Study questions from a single subject or a mixture of all four
- Get detailed feedback on your performance and a full user history
- Answers are fully explained and cross-referenced to the Blackstone's Police Manuals so you can easily go back and revise the relevant subject area

Subscriptions: **£95.00** (12 months) | **£75.00** (8 months) | **£50.00** (3 months)

Blackstone's Police Manuals 2008 and Q&As 2008 Online*

- The essential integrated study package for all police officers sitting the Part 1 promotion examinations
- The ONLY service to provide direct links from the detailed answers in Blackstone's Police Q&As Online to the relevant section of the Blackstone's Police Manuals Online

Subscriptions: **£150.00** (12 months) | **£120.00** (8 months)

For more information and subscription details, please visit **www.blackstonespolice.com**

** Please note: the Blackstone's Police Q&As Online service is not endorsed by the NPIA*

ALBQ&AA08

Also available to help with your revision

Blackstone's Police Sergeants' and Inspectors' Mock Examination Paper 2008*

Paul Connor, *Police Training Consultant*

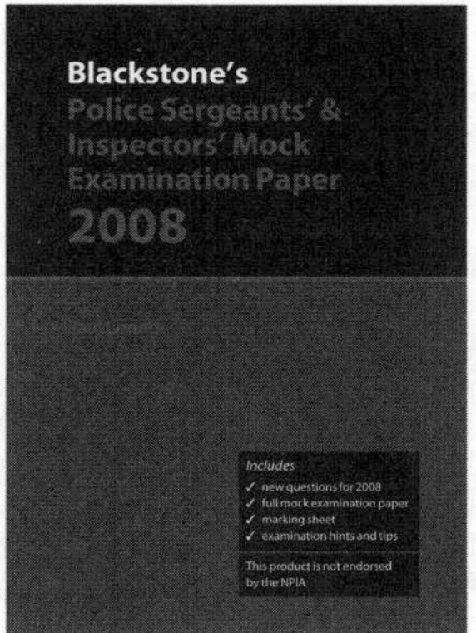

'Hits straight at the heart of the matter in a no nonsense fashion.'

Detective Sergeant Simon Davies, West Mercia Police

'The student will learn not only the answers, but also the process by using this product.'

Detective Sergeant Phil Stokoe, Durham Police

Minimise last-minute panic and increase your confidence with this one-stop resource for examination technique and practice.

- The mock paper is one of the best ways to prepare for the Sergeants' Part I exam.
- Candidates can experience the same structure and timing of the exam by answering 150 questions in 3 hours.
- Completely updated for 2008 to cover all recent legislative developments including the Fraud Act 2006, the Emergency Workers (Obstruction) Act 2006, the Safeguarding Vulnerable Groups Act 2006 and the Police and Justice Act 2006.

Blackstone's Police Sergeants' and Inspectors' Mock Examination Paper 2008 features a selection of multiple-choice questions set by an experienced question writer. Designed for use in simulated exam conditions, it will test your knowledge and understanding of the law, and your ability to answer questions under pressure.

The mock examination paper is accompanied by detailed marking matrices; allowing you to calculate your overall percentage score and recognise the areas you need to focus on. Learn where your areas of strength and weakness lie, and channel your revision into the most productive areas of the syllabus.

Applicable to the Sergeants' Part I promotion exam in March 2008 and the Inspectors' exam in September 2008.

For more information on this, and other Police books from Blackstone's, please visit **www.oup.co.uk/law/police**

£15.99 Available from all good bookshops

October 2007 | 110 pages | Paperback | 978-0-19-923141-6

** Please note: this product is not endorsed by the NPIA*

ALBQ&AB08